Christy is able to unpack the stories of these five women in a way that is both relatable and accessible to us all. We can easily see ourselves in each woman. Their struggles and shortcomings, their doubts and dreams, and their victories and defeats remind us we are not alone. A great reminder to us all of the love of God that redeems and transforms.

—Dr. Lori Salierno-Maldonado
Founder and CEO of Teach One to Lead One

Not only are women the incubators of human life, but we are also the sustainers, teachers, and influencers of those whom we raise. Christy has taken the lives of pock-marked women and restored their stories through grace, love, and dignity. Furthermore, she teaches others the power of redemption and the beauty that comes afterwards.

—Bianca Juarez Olthoff
Speaker, Author, and Chief Storyteller for A21

In a world that demands perfection, Christy addresses the real issue we all face: accepting God's work of redemption in our lives, believing that He continually brings beauty out of ashes. Christy's words are important and life-giving for women at any stage.

—Bonnie Lewis
Director of Research at EvFree Fullerton and Author at findtheblue.com

Whatever Christy does she does with all her heart and *Reclaimed* is an example of her commitment to do her work as "unto the Lord." Others will be challenged and encouraged by the words and wisdom of this study of five women of God found in the genealogy of Jesus.

—Gary Damore
Ed.D., Educator

Reclaimed

• Uncovering Your Worth •

A Study Of Five Women In The Lineage Of Jesus

CHRISTY FAY

HIGHERLIFE
PUBLISHING & MARKETING
www.ahigherlife.com

Oviedo, Florida

Reclaimed—Uncovering Your Worth
Copyright © 2015 by Christy Fay

Unless otherwise noted, Scripture quotations are taken from *The Holy Bible, New International Version*®. NIV® Copyright © 1973, 1978, 1984, 2011 by Biblica, Inc.® Used by permission. All rights reserved worldwide.

Scripture references marked NLT are taken from *The Holy Bible: New Living Translation.* Copyright © 1996, 2004, 2007, 2013 by Tyndale House Foundation. Used by permission of Tyndale House Publishers Inc., Carol Stream, Illinois 60188. All rights reserved.

Scripture references marked MSG are taken from *The Message* by Eugene H. Peterson. Copyright © 1993, 1994, 1995, 1996, 2000, 2001, 2002.

Scripture quotations marked KJV are taken from the King James Version of the Bible. Copyright © 1982 by Thomas Nelson,Inc. Used by permission. All rights reserved.

Scripture quotations marked ESV are from The Holy Bible, English Standard Version® (ESV®), copyright © 2001 by Crossway, a publishing ministry of Good News Publishers. Used by permission. All rights reserved.

ISBN: 978-0-9907578-7-0

Published by HigherLife Development Services, Inc.
HigherLife Development Services, Inc.
100 Alexandria Blvd. Suite 9
Oviedo, Florida 32765
www.ahigherlife.com

Printed in South Korea.

DEDICATION

*To my dearest Nona, we lost you this
year, so that you might join Him.*

*There is no way to count the ways
you made each of us better.*

*You, a loving wife, a devoted mother, a teacher, a writer, an
amazing grandmother, and great-grandmother. You wore
love, and you wore it well. I think of Colossians 3:14.*

The words of this book are for you.

May they honor your life and your memory.

CONTENTS

CONTEXT: ABOUT THIS STUDY 1

WEEK ONE—SUBTEXT: FIVE WOMEN IN THE LINEAGE OF JESUS

Day One: Relative 8

Day Two: A Divine Invitation 18

Day Three: Everyone's In 24

Day Four: Firm Foundation 29

Day Five: Keeping Account 35

WEEK TWO—PERIPETEIA: TAMAR

Day One: Litmus Test 46

Day Two: Clearing the Air 51

Day Three: Impossible Circumstances 56

Day Four: Conflict Resolution 62

Day Five: Shame, Blame, Cover, Hide, and Run 67

WEEK THREE—OXYMORON: RAHAB

Day One: Coincidence or Divine Providence? 76

Day Two: How Stalks and Flax Changed Everything 81

Day Three: When the King's on Your Doorstep 88

Day Four: *That* God, *My* God 93

Day Five: A Red Cord 97

WEEK FOUR—FORESHADOWING: RUTH

Day One: Naomi 106

Day Two: The Impressive Résumé of Boaz 112

Day Three: All that You Say, I Will Do 119

Day Four: Is He Worthy 125

Day Five: Empty to Full 130

WEEK FIVE—EPITHET: URIAH'S WIFE

Day One: In Step 136

Day Two: Two Words that Changed Everything 141

Day Three: The Pollution of Ingratitude 146

Day Four: Reaping What We Sow 152

Day Five: Legacy 158

WEEK SIX—RISING ACTION: MARY

Day One: May Your Words to Me Be Fulfilled 168

Day Two: He Has Done Great Things 175

Day Three: Great is Your Faithfulness 179

Day Four: And a Sword Will Pierce Your Own Soul 185

Day Five: Ponder 191

SMALL GROUP DISCUSSION GUIDE 199

SCRIPTURE MEMORIZATION 207

Context

ABOUT THIS STUDY

Welcome. If you are reading this, you have decided to embark on a new study by an author you probably do not know. Thanks for taking a risk. I am a mother, a wife, a daughter, a friend, and now, I guess I get to call myself a writer. You may not know me, but I have prayed for you. As I've sat down to write and to study, you have been on my heart. I am grateful for each and every one of you and can't wait for what the upcoming weeks will hold for us. I have completed this study on the cusp of finishing Beth Moore's *Children of the Day*. The words of 1 Thessalonians are fresh in my mind, "…we loved you so much, we were delighted to share with you not only the gospel of God but our lives as well" (1 Thessalonians 2:8 NIV). You will find that in these pages I have shared, not only the gospel, but also pieces of my life. As we begin, I want to answer some questions that I would have if I were in your shoes.

What did I get myself into?

I love old stuff. I guess the proper term would be antiques, but even that seems more polished than I'd like. I'm not sure the beat-up old shutters and window frames that I have hung all over my house would really qualify as antiques. They're just flat out old, used, dilapidated, and run down. Nevertheless, I love them.

One of my most favorite places in my home is our office. Well, I shouldn't call it an office. It's a wall that stretches about twelve feet across with a desk pushed against it. My mother crafted the desk with her own hands, and it runs the entire length of the wall. That wall holds some of my most treasured items. There's an old shutter that is not only interesting to look at, but serves the practical purpose of housing in its crevices our household bills and other important papers. Then there's a big iron architectural piece—a metal grid, I guess, for lack of a better way to describe it. I have no idea of its past use, but I have chosen to hang little boxes, crates, and clip-boards from its crisscrossing bars. Next is a funky clock, which holds for me nostalgic value, as Michael and I purchased it from Pottery Barn with a gift card we received as a wedding gift. It's one of the only pieces of wall art we still have displayed from our early-married days. It's funny how our tastes and styles have morphed and changed over our near ten years of marriage. There are old books in my office, with pages torn and yellowed front covers peeling back. My wall also hold old medicine cabinets that we have stripped down for housing canisters of crayons, erasers, pencils, and markers. One of my favorite parts of this collage are the large letters representing the first initial of each of my children's names.

I love this little spot in my house because we all end up in there, for one reason or another. I often sit at my laptop, with my Bible and books strewn all over the place, writing and studying. My kids can be found perched on their chairs, doing homework or creating some kind of artistic masterpiece. My husband will likely be working at his baking station, a gift my mom and I gave him for his birthday one year, because in this house, my man does all the baking—and he's a legit baker. When he's behind the stand-up mixer, step away, folks! There we all are, amidst these old relics, once considered junk and tossed aside, now used as the platform for inspiration, creation, and innovation. The old becomes new in this space. The ugly becomes beautiful. And the once judged useless is transformed into something worthwhile once more.

It's a wonderful little nook not just because of what memories are made there, but because of the metaphor it represents. Those items were disheveled, bedraggled, and written off as worthless junk, but with a little tender loving care, some imagination, and a whole lot of hard work, a new day has dawned for them. This is the story of the Bible. Messed up, mistaken, riddled, marred, corrupted, and damaged as we are, God sees something else. He sees potential. He sees a new story being written. A new creation rising from the rubble. And that, dear sisters, is what this Bible study is about. Our God is able, and He has promised to take His very broken people and use them to fix a despairing and broken world. This is the good news of the gospel; it is the story of the Bible. It is never too late for you. You are never too damaged or beyond the reach of His merciful hand. His desire is for each of you to step into the new creation that you already are and learn to live comfortably in it until your whole identity is defined by what He sees when He looks upon you, instead of what you see.

God instructed the prophet Jeremiah to go down to the house of a potter to receive a message. This is what the text says, "This is the word that came to Jeremiah from the Lord: 'Go down to the potter's house, and there I will give you my message.' So I went down to the potter's house, and I saw him working at the wheel. But the pot he was shaping from the clay was marred in his hands; so the potter formed it into another pot, shaping it as seemed best to him" (Jeremiah 18:1–4 NIV). God goes on to address the Israelites through the prophet Jeremiah. "Then the word of the Lord came to me. He said, 'Can I not do with you, Israel, as this potter does?' declares the Lord. 'Like clay in the hand of the potter, so are you in my hand, Israel'" (Jeremiah 18:5–6 NIV).

The people of Israel, God's people, were merely clay in the Master Potter's hands. Today, we, still His people, are the same. "For we are God's masterpiece," Paul wrote in his letter to the Ephesians, "He has created us anew in Christ Jesus, so we can do the good things he planned for us long ago" (Ephesians 2:10 NLT).

This study is all about being clay. It's about recognizing our worth as God's masterpiece; it's about a new story unfolding and continually being crafted by the Master Storyteller Himself.

The next six weeks will open up a journey for us. My hope, my prayer, and the deepest longing of my heart is that you might discover just how profoundly valuable your story is. And that you would discover your worth, simply and solely in a God who desires to write something new—something more beautiful and eloquent than you could ever have dreamed. Get ready to be reclaimed!

How does this study work?

We begin our study in Matthew 1 with the genealogy of Jesus. An interesting and curious place to begin, I realize, but our focus will quickly narrow to the five women tucked into this long list. Our first week will serve as an overview to the genealogy, subsequently leading us to unpack some of our own lineage and histories. We will discover how our past can have some level of influence over our future. After that, it's one woman per week of study. Each of these women's stories will lead us, guide us, and, hopefully, inspire us to a renewed vision as we live out our own stories.

Each week has five days of homework. I am a mother of four, so I understand being short on time. It is also my job to challenge you, so, if you read "five days of homework" and already your palms are getting sweaty and if you're thinking, "there's no way I can do that," let me assure you, you are capable of more than you think. If you think you can do one day of homework a week, try to do two. If you think you might be able to do three, aim for the skies and set your goal to five.

When I shared the news with some of my dear Bible study women that I was writing my own study, they asked, "How in the world are you going to find time for that?"

I said two words: "Nap time!"

As many days as I could, while at least some of my kids were down to rest, I ran to my desk, sat down, studied, and wrote. On some days, all I could get out was a few paragraphs; on others, it was a page or more. I found that investing small amounts of time added up to something bigger. Sooner than I thought, I bragged to my husband, "I have fifty pages."

Then it was seventy-five, and then one hundred. The bottom line? We women are the best at multitasking than any other species on the planet by far. I guarantee it. You've got this. Spending time in God's Word will never disappoint. The words, labored over and written in this study, are not mine. They are His. I have never been more certain of anything in my life. If you open your hearts, I know He will show up.

Video Session One
INTRODUCTION/STORY

INTRODUCTION

The five women in the Lineage of Jesus are Tamar, _____, Ruth, Bathsheba, and _____.

The definition of reclaimed is to demand the return or _____ of, as a right, a possession.

MATTHEW VS. LUKE

The gospel of Matthew mainly differs from the other Gospels due to its heavily Jewish perspective. He also quotes the _____ _____ more than any of the other Gospels. He spends a great deal of time pointing out the references from the Torah present in Jesus's _____.

Luke is a _____Greek_____ _____Doctor_____.

Christy's theory as to why Matthew and Luke's gospel accounts are different:

_____

_____

_____

MATTHEW'S STORY (MATTHEW 9:9–13)

"Go figure out what this Scripture means: 'I'm after mercy, not _____.'
I'm here to invite outsiders, not _____ insiders" (Matthew 9:13 MSG).

The Greek word for *mercy* is _____.

Strong's Bible Dictionary defines the word as follows: "*Eleos* is the free gift for the forgiveness of sins and is related to the _____ sins brings. God's tender sense of our misery displays itself in His efforts to lessen and entirely

Mercy becomes the medicine that Matthew so desperately needs to remove His misery. And these five women in the genealogy are in need of this same medicine.

God speaks over us: "I will have _____." (Matthew 9:13 KJV) We in turn can speak, "I will have mercy," into the lives of those around us.

What does this mean for me?

Week One

SUBTEXT: FIVE WOMEN IN THE LINEAGE OF JESUS

[suhb-tekst]

noun

   1.
the underlying or implicit meaning, as of a
literary work.

Day One
RELATIVE

If you're a hard worker and do a good job, you deserve your pay; we don't call your wages a gift. But if you see that the job is too big for you, that it's something only God can do, and you trust him to do it—you could never do it for yourself no matter how hard and long you worked—well, that trusting-him-to-do-it is what gets you set right with God, by God. Sheer gift (Romans 4: 4–5 MSG).

I love the Bible. I realize that statement may come across as nerdy, but I really do. I love the black ink, the letters formed to make words and sentences. I especially love the red ink—the words that Jesus actually spoke at one time or another. God Himself, in the flesh, arrived on the scene and spoke audible words. And we can now read this collection of stories, which reveals the character and heart of God, the One who spoke the world into existence!

I read many years ago that if you find yourself interested and intrigued by this Jesus you've heard spoken about, the best thing to do is to simply open the Bible and start reading. Even if you possess no background knowledge or understanding of anything religious or spiritual and even if the thought of reading this ancient text intimidates you to no end, swallow your fears and give it a shot. A good place to start is with the Gospels. Just open up to one of those four accounts, Matthew, Mark, Luke, or John, and read. Rebecca Manley Piper, author of *Out of the Salt Shaker and into the World*, said, "Once you read something that strikes you as interesting, something that stands out, try to immediately put it into practice. You may not understand it fully or grasp its profundity by simply reading it, but by acting on the words, you will catch a glimpse of a God alive and working not just thousands of years ago, but today."

That thought has stuck with me. I think there is a universal truth in it. Timothy would say it this way, "All Scripture is God breathed and is useful for teaching, rebuking, correcting and training in righteousness, so that the servant of God may be thoroughly equipped for every good work" (2 Timothy 3:16–17 NIV). I believe this is true. I believe it with the entirety of who I am. In my heart, I know that God is alive and at work and that with His Word, He brings clarity, peace, hope, truth, understanding, wisdom, and everything in between. I would say this is true of almost every part of the Holy Scriptures, with the exception of maybe Matthew 1 (or so I thought). Turn there and you will see a long list of names. Names that are mostly archaic and outdated.

"What is this for?," I wondered. Maybe you are wrestling with the same question. Perhaps the first sixteen verses could be used as sort of guide to "holy" baby names—useful to parents expecting their first child. Of course, Amminadab and Nahshon aren't exactly on the top of the list for anyone, I wouldn't think. There are a few names that might be familiar—Abraham, Isaac, and David—but smashed in between the recognizable ones are a bunch of obscure ones, with very little, if any, meaning to us. How could this list help us live better? How could this list of names lead us to more peace, knowledge, and wisdom in our lives?

I noticed that sandwiched in between all those men were five women. "What were *they* doing there?," I wondered. In an ancient culture that placed men on a pedestal and where there was usually no room for anything remotely female, their names were etched permanently onto the page. Mathew, the author of this gospel account, who we know was a tax collector before receiving his call to come and follow Jesus, was also a Jew and was writing this story for those who called themselves Jews as well.

His hope was to present an overwhelming amount of evidence—enough to prove without a doubt that Jesus was in fact the King of the Jews. Reaching back into the Old Testament, he quoted the prophets who had predicted that a king would come riding on a donkey and be born to a virgin. It was absolutely critical for Matthew's readers to see that Jesus descended from King David and from the first Jew, Abraham. These two men, specifically, added fuel to the fire of his argument.

It's important to see Jesus in the context of His Jewish history, but what about the presence of five women? Matthew's decision to include Tamar, Rahab, Ruth, the wife of Uriah, and Mary tells me there is another story being told. It is that story I am most interested in.

There is no other way to begin this journey together than to start with the text itself. It should always take preeminence in its rightful role as "a lamp for my feet, a light on my path" (Psalm 119:105 NIV). I warn you, the first seventeen verses of Matthew are far from exhilarating, but take the time to read them now.

> This is the genealogy of Jesus the Messiah the son of David, the
>   son of Abraham:
> Abraham was the father of Isaac,
>   Isaac the father of Jacob,
>   Jacob the father of Judah and his brothers,
>   Judah the father of Perez and Zerah, whose mother was
>   Tamar,
>   Perez the father of Hezron,
>   Hezron the father of Ram,
>   Ram the father of Amminadab,
>   Amminadab the father of Nahshon,
>   Nahshon the father of Salmon,
>   Salmon the father of Boaz, whose mother was Rahab,
>   Boaz the father of Obed, whose mother was Ruth,
>   Obed the father of Jesse,
>   and Jesse the father of King David.
>   David was the father of Solomon, whose mother had been
>   Uriah's wife,
>   Solomon the father of Rehoboam,
>   Rehoboam the father of Abijah,
>   Abijah the father of Asa,
>   Asa the father of Jehoshaphat,
>   Jehoshaphat the father of Jehoram,

> Jehoram the father of Uzziah,
> Uzziah the father of Jotham,
> Jotham the father of Ahaz,
> Ahaz the father of Hezekiah,
> Hezekiah the father of Manasseh,
> Manasseh the father of Amon,
> Amon the father of Josiah,
> and Josiah the father of Jeconiah and his brothers at the
>   time of the exile to Babylon.
> After the exile to Babylon:
> Jeconiah was the father of Shealtiel,
> Shealtiel the father of Zerubbabel,
> Zerubbabel the father of Abihud,
> Abihud the father of Eliakim,
> Eliakim the father of Azor,
> Azor the father of Zadok,
> Zadok the father of Akim,
> Akim the father of Elihud,
> Elihud the father of Eleazar,
> Eleazar the father of Matthan,
> Matthan the father of Jacob,
> and Jacob the father of Joseph, the husband of Mary, and
>   Mary was the mother of Jesus who is called the Messiah.

Thus there were fourteen generations in all from Abraham to David, fourteen from David to the exile to Babylon, and fourteen from the exile to the Messiah (Matthew 1:1–17 NIV).

What do you know about your own family history (country of origin, religious orientation, etc.)?

_____

_____

_____

We all have a tendency to take extra pride in those relatives from our lineage that may be considered famous or even royal. Is there someone in your family tree that you, or your family, take a special interest in? If so, why might that be?

_____

_____

_____

It's human, isn't it? We all like to boast about anyone that seems to boost the overall morale and heighten the reputation of our familial identity. By stating our relationship, we take part in their accomplishments and claim them to some extent as our own even though that person may have lived hundreds and hundreds of years before we were even born. My husband's family members are convinced that John Tyler, the tenth president of the United States, is a part of their lineage and will eagerly point that out to anyone who asks about their history.

On the flip side, we are also quick to shove under the rug any generations that might have disgraced the family referring to them as black sheep. Clearly, that person or persons were just the exception to the rule of an otherwise superlative lineage. As we reflect on the genealogy in Matthew's gospel, it's curious to ponder why certain names were included and others left out. In verse 1, he mentions two major players in biblical history. Who are they?

_____

_____

What, if anything, do you know about these two men that would clue us in as to why Matthew mentions them?

_____

_____

_____

_____

Let's focus our attention first on David. He was and still is a pretty big deal in Jewish history. We glean some insight about who he was and why his name is featured prominently in this genealogy by looking in 2 Samuel. "I will be his father, and he will be my son. If he sins, I will correct and discipline him with the rod, like any father would do. But my favor will not be taken from him as I took it from Saul, whom I removed from your sight. Your house and your kingdom will continue before me for all time, and your throne will be secure forever" (2 Samuel 7:14–16 NLT).

What does verse 16 say about the kingdom of David?

_____

_____

The promise made in 2 Samuel 7:14–16, which is often referred to as the prophecy of the seed of David, guarantees that David's house and kingdom (his family tree) will endure forever. You might wonder how this is possible. David is just a man, and subject to the laws of the universe like anyone else. How could he escape death? In Isaiah 9, the prophet speaks of a child that will be born in the coming years. "For to us a child is born, to us a son is given, and the government will be on his shoulders. And he will be called Wonderful Counselor, Mighty God, Everlasting Father, Prince of Peace" (Isaiah 9:6 NIV). This may seem like an obvious question, but to what child is this verse referring?

_____

_____

The prophet Isaiah continues, "Of the greatness of his government and peace there will be no end. He will reign on David's throne and over his kingdom, establishing and upholding it with justice and righteousness from that time on and forever. The zeal of the Lord Almighty will accomplish this" (Isaiah 9:7 NIV). Who will reign on David's throne?

_____

_____

What are the characteristics of that reign?

_____

_____

_____

_____

Matthew, when he mentions David in his genealogy, does so knowing that his readers, many of whom are very familiar with the verses that we just looked at, will immediately understand the connection he is making. Jesus, the Son of David, is in fact the rightful heir to the throne. He is the Messiah, the One they have waited for, the One who will rule with justice and righteousness both now and forever.

Let's move on to our second major player. If you recall from above, his name is Abraham. Matthew also calls Jesus, the Son of Abraham. I'd like to take a closer look at why this title might be significant. Genesis states, "I will make you into a great nation, and I will bless you; I will make your name great, and you will be a blessing. I will bless those who bless you, and whoever curses you I will curse; and all peoples on earth will be blessed through you" (Genesis 12: 2–3 NIV). Is this promise only for a specific group of people or for all people?

_____

_____

God promises that through Abraham *all* people will be blessed. Let's ask ourselves what being blessed means. To help in answering this question, look up Romans 4:1–8. According to verse 6, *blessedness* comes to the one whom God what?

_____

The phrase "credited as righteousness" comes up a lot in the book of Romans but it can be a somewhat elusive phrase. What does it mean that Abraham was credited as righteous?

_____

In its original translation, that word *righteous* came out of the context of the Jewish court system. Those reading it at the time in which Paul, the author of Romans, was writing would have interpreted it through this lens. In the Jewish legal system, there were three parties: the judge, the plaintiff, and the defendant. There were no attorneys prosecuting for each side as we have today. Each party presented their case to one judge. Judges were required to take an oath of office before being sworn in just as they do today, but the judges of Paul's time entered into a covenant—one that called them to govern impartially, punishing wrongdoing, and supporting the cause of the defenseless. A judge who adhered to this covenant showed his faithfulness, or his righteousness, to the covenant. The judge could not impute his or her own righteous character onto the plaintiff or defendant. He could only hear the case and declare one of the two parties *righteous*. As N.T. Wright comments, "righteousness—not morally good and deserving of a favorable outcome, but one who is given the status by the court as one 'being in the right' as a result of the judge's decision.

What does this mean as we examine this word in the context of Romans and Abraham? God, who is the judge, hears the case, or cries, of Israel as they continually call out to Him to rescue them from their enemies. God remains faithful to the covenant, or the promise, He made to Abraham. Once He rules, the verdict is out. He makes us righteous. Not by transferring His righteous character to us, not because we are morally good or deserving, but simply in the ruling itself. Remember we learned in Genesis 15:7 that God would bless Abraham and that blessing came as a result of Abraham being credited as righteous. The good news that Paul shares in the first part of Romans 4 is that we too inherit this blessing through Abraham. We, too, are "credited as righteous."

Let's continue to look at Romans 4:

> Now, is this blessing only for the Jews, or is it also for uncircumcised Gentiles? Well, we have been saying that Abraham was counted as righteous by God because of his faith. But how did this happen? Was he counted as righteous only after he was circumcised, or was it before he was circumcised? Clearly, God accepted Abraham before he was circumcised!
>
> Circumcision was a sign that Abraham already had faith and that God had already accepted him and declared him to be righteous—even before he was circumcised. So Abraham is the spiritual father of those who have faith but have not been circumcised. They are counted as righteous because of their faith. And Abraham is also the spiritual father of those who have been circumcised, but only if they have the same kind of faith Abraham had before he was circumcised.
>
> Clearly, God's promise to give the whole earth to Abraham and his descendants was based not on his obedience to God's law, but on a right relationship with God that comes by faith. If God's promise is only for those who obey the law, then faith is not necessary and the promise is pointless. For the law always brings punishment on those who try to obey it. (The only way to avoid breaking the law is to have no law to break!)
>
> So the promise is received by faith. It is given as a free gift. And we are all certain to receive it, whether or not we live according to the law of Moses, if we have faith like Abrahamfa. For Abraham is the father of all who believe (Romans 4:9–16 NLT).

We learn in this chapter that "blessedness" is not just for the circumcised (of course, he is speaking of the Jews), but also for the _____ (Gentiles).

Let's go back to the original question. With your newfound knowledge of the Jewish court system, why do you think Matthew felt it was important to call Jesus the Son of Abraham?

_____

_____

_____

Jesus is the reason the covenant made with Abraham can be fulfilled. Through Him, the richest of God's blessings can be poured out. We are *all* made right, "credited as righteous," by the faithful Judge.

Abraham is considered, by many scholars, to be the first converted Gentile, and so Matthew's mention of him, in the very beginning of his genealogy, points to a theme we will see through the remainder of the chapter and the entirety of the gospel. This good news, this gracious verdict of right standing, is not just for the Jews, but for the Gentiles too.

Day Two

A DIVINE INVITATION

Instead, immense in mercy and with an incredible love, he embraced us. He took our sin-dead lives and made us alive in Christ. He did all this on his own, with no help from us! (Ephesians 2:4–5 MSG).

Today, we are going to begin with a question. If you would, answer the following and treat it as a sort of warm-up to today's lesson. In fact, this question will prepare us for the remaining days of this week's study. Have you ever received news that shocked or surprised you, something extremely unexpected, or something positive or negative that ultimately altered the course of your future in some way? What happened?

_____

_____

_____

_____

Hold on to that thought as we move through the rest of our material. We will come back to it at the end of Day 4.

We've just taken some time to examine two important men mentioned in the beginning of Matthew's genealogy. But Tamar, Rahab, Ruth, the wife of Uriah, and Mary are the five women listed there. Later, we'll read the details of each of their stories. For now, let's examine what it is that these five women might have in common. Let's turn in our Bibles and read Genesis 38:1–6.

Verse 6 tells us "And Judah took a wife for Er his firstborn, and her name was Tamar" (ESV). Judging from verse 2, what nationality was Tamar?

_____

_____

We would assume from the text that Tamar was a Canaanite, but that is really all we could conclude. It does not give us any further detail about her heritage. However, Philo, a Jewish exegete who lived at the time of Matthew fills in some of the gaps: "Tamar was a woman from Syria Palestine who had been bred up in her own native city, which was devoted to the worship of many gods, being full of statues, and images, and, in short, of idols of every kind and description."

For those reading Matthew's gospel, Syria Palestine was undoubtedly Gentile. This allows us to conclude that Tamar is a Gentile herself. It is here that we stumble on this word *Gentile* for the first time. What does it mean to be a Gentile? The dictionary defines this word as not Jewish.

If you are reading this and have never, either by birth or by religious preference, considered yourself a Jew, then you are a Gentile.

Let's take a look at our next female listed, Rahab. Read Joshua 2:1. According to this passage, where was Rahab from?

Jericho was considered one of the strongest fortresses in the land of Canaan and therefore the very first city that was conquered with God's help in the Promised Land. Jericho's location in the land of Canaan allows us to say with certainty, that Rahab was, like Tamar, a Gentile.

In Ruth 1:1–4 we discover where Ruth was from. Read these verses and record your findings below.

_____

_____

_____

Moab is the name given to the eldest son of Lot, the nephew of Abraham. As noted in Genesis 19:37 he was born of Lot and one of his own daughters (yes, you read that right). "The older daughter had a son, and she named him Moab, he is the father of the Moabites today" (NIV). With an incestuous relationship as this nation's origin, we can easily infer that Moab is a Gentile nation. Of course, further deducing that Ruth is also a Gentile. Are you sensing an overall pattern emerging?

The fourth woman listed is the wife of Uriah. Read 2 Samuel 11:2–3 and answer the following questions:

What is the wife of Uriah's actual name?

_____

What nationality is given for Uriah?

_____

I can vividly remember being asked when my husband and I were in premarital counseling with our pastor, "When, at the end of the ceremony, I announce you, do you want me to say, 'Mr. and Mrs. Michael Fay' or 'Mr. and Mrs. Michael and Christy Fay'?"

That was a no-brainer for me. I went with the latter. I mean, I was overjoyed to be getting married and all, but I had already given up my last name—a name I'd possessed for twenty-one years and one that was a part of me. I did not want to give up my first name, too. When I read the portion of Matthew's genealogy where he said, "And David was the father of Solomon by the wife of Uriah" (Genesis 1:6 ESV), I feel a little offended. She was the mother of the wisest man that ever lived and all she got was "the wife of Uriah"?! Why would Matthew have done it this way? Nothing is really ever an accident, especially in the Word of God, but it does beg the question, "Why?" Most scholars believe that by omitting her actual name, which was Bathsheba, it placed emphasis on her origin. The Hittites were among the seven nations that God's people, when inhabiting the Promised Land, were to drive out (Deuteronomy 7:1, 20:17). The Hittite nation was pretty much as Gentile as you could get, and so, I'm sure I don't have to point out that Bathsheba (I'll call her by her actual name) was a Gentile. Matthew, by calling her the wife of Uriah, wants there to be no mistaking that.

This brings us to the very last woman on our list, Mary. The four women mentioned up until this point were Gentile. Mary is the exception to the rule. Read Luke 1:27 and write down any facts we learn about her from this text.

_____

_____

_____

Although it doesn't say it directly, we do know that Mary was from the tribe of Judah and that she was connected by marriage to Elizabeth, John the Baptist's mother, who was from the tribe of Aaron. From first glance, she seems to be a better fit into the genealogy of Jesus. And when I say better fit, I mean, she's with the "in crowd." She is a Jew, and the type of woman Matthew's reader might have expected to find in the first chapter of his book. However, she does have one thing in common with the other four. Her name would have been synonymous with some amount of scandal. When we are first introduced to her, she is found to be "with child" before actually walking down the aisle with her betrothed.

Judging by these five women's histories, lineage, and stories, they don't seem a natural fit for the Savior of the world's genealogy. They are marked and they are unclean by Jewish standards. They are far from perfect, and yet, there they are in black and white. There is no amount of white out that can remove them from the role they play in God's story. I don't know about you, but by nature I like things all wrapped up and tied with a bow. I like things that are clean and shiny. I don't want toilet paper hanging out of my dress or the middle button on my shirt undone, especially if I'm meeting someone for the first time. If I were Matthew, writing the first chapter of my book and making my first impression, I would have passed over these women. No one would have noticed if they weren't included, right? But Matthew, under the guidance of the Holy Spirit, chose otherwise. He not only included them, but did so with a certain amount of pride. Remember we learned he wrote "wife of Uriah," not to hide her lineage, but to highlight it. He wants his Jewish readers to know that these *Gentile women* (being female and Gentile was kind of like having two strikes against you) belong in this lineage and in the story that God is telling.

I wish I could see through the pages and look directly into your eyes. I wish I could hold your hands in mine. I wish we could be together, face-to-face, because there is no amount of bolding or italics that can help me emphasize enough what I am about to write. These women belong in the story God is telling. And, *so do you*! There is a genealogy being written right now. The story God is telling is not finished. It's a work in progress. And His story is meant to involve you. You may not feel worthy. You might feel like the mistakes you've made and the person you are disqualifies you from participation in His divine novel. Let me assure you, and even more so, let God Himself assure you: the invitation is and forever will, remain open. Read Ephesians 2:1–10 as you conclude your study today. Meditate on it. Reflect on it. Let it get inside of you and breathe life into you. God is inviting you in. Will you accept His invitation today?

It wasn't so long ago that you were mired in that old stagnant life of sin. You let the world, which doesn't know the first thing about living, tell you how to live. You filled your lungs with polluted unbelief, and then exhaled disobedience. We all did it, all of us doing what we felt like doing, when we felt like doing it, all of us in the same boat. It's a wonder God didn't lose his temper and do away with the whole lot of us. Instead, immense in mercy and with an incredible love, he embraced us. He took our sin-dead lives and made us alive in Christ. He did all this on his own, with no help from us! Then he picked us up and set us down in highest heaven in company with Jesus, our Messiah.

Now God has us where he wants us, with all the time in this world and the next to shower grace and kindness upon us in Christ Jesus. Saving is all his idea, and all his work. All we do is trust him enough to let him do it. It's God's gift from start to finish! We don't play the major role. If we did, we'd probably go around bragging that we'd done the whole thing! No, we neither make nor save ourselves. God does both the making and saving. He creates each of us by Christ Jesus to join him in the work he does, the good work he has gotten ready for us to do, work we had better be doing (Ephesians 2:1–10 MSG).

Day Three

EVERYONE'S IN

Do not call anything impure that God has made clean (Acts 10:15 NLT).

Let's entertain a thought that we have been working up to in yesterday's homework. It is certainly easy, in today's time, to open the first chapter of Matthew and read this long and boring list of names. Then, to arrive at the female names, pause for a brief moment, and ponder why those names are there. It makes sense to skim ahead to the better parts—the parts where Jesus walks on water and makes a guy's hand grow back. Those are the cool parts, after all. For Matthew's readers, first century Jews, this list, and especially the women included, would have been truly *shocking*— and that's an understatement. For thousands and thousands of years the Jews had been told, you are a holy people, a people set apart, you are to live differently, live by your own sets of rules and standards, eat different things, don't intermarry, and keep your family line pure and unpolluted. And there they are: Tamar, Rahab, Ruth, the wife of Uriah, and Mary. They must have thought, surely, this is a mistake.

Maybe some of you can relate to these Jewish readers. Glance back to the answer you recorded at the beginning of yesterday's lesson. We've all had our share of shocking news. Sometimes this news comes to us like an unexpected, but ultimately wonderful, surprise, like an unplanned pregnancy or unforeseen, but enriching, friendship. Sometimes shocking news brings with it a shadow that feels oppressive and overwhelming, like a cancer diagnosis or a sudden death.

As we are still getting to know one another, I'll share with you the first time this question surfaced for me. I'll never forget when my mom and dad told me we would be moving from Toronto, Canada to Scottsdale, Arizona. I was ten and living in a city I called home, in a school I loved, and surrounded by an awesome group of girlfriends. I remember thinking, "Arizona, what's in Arizona?" Driving through Scottsdale on our way to the home we had rented on a scouting trip a few months before the big move, I thought, "Wow, this is actually a normal city, with regular buildings and sidewalks!"

In my head, I had pictured Arizona like an old Western movie—or perhaps even more like the movie, *Maverick,* the one with Mel Gibson and Jodie Foster. I expected to see dirt streets and saloons with swinging doors in the front. In my heart of hearts, I was hoping for some kind of live gunfight. With that first drive through the state, my hopes for this kind of action were dashed. Nevertheless, I did conclude that with this move, my life was going to be rather different from before.

Let's take a moment and read the story in Acts 10:9–23. While it may seem strange to you at first, our main character is a man named Peter who had some revolutionary news delivered to him. Let's take a few minutes to work through this peculiar dream that Peter has. He sees heaven open and something come down from heaven. What is it?

_____

_____

Read Revelation 7:1. What might the four corners of the linen sheet refer to?

_____

_____

If you said the four corners of the earth, you are right. It appears that this trance or "vision" Peter is having is one that extends to the whole world.

_____

In verse 12 of Acts 10, we are told that the sheet contains _____ kinds of four footed animals as well as reptiles and birds. Judging from Peter's response, are there clean, unclean, or both types of animals present?

_____

In Leviticus 11, you will find a very detailed list of what kinds of animals were considered unclean and all sorts of rituals and rules regarding how to proceed if one happens to become "unclean." I will not ask you to read this whole chapter as it does not hold a whole lot of value for most of us now. If, of course, this perks your interest, go ahead and read it. Verse 44 gives the reason that God has put this list of regulations. What is it?

_____

_____

For all of Peter's life, and most likely the lives of his father, and his father's father, and his father's father's father (you get the point), those foods that were considered unclean had been avoided like the plague. No Jew, and Peter was no exception, would have wanted to risk becoming "ritually defiled" and be unable to come into God's presence in worship. Perhaps that is why when God says "Get up, Peter. Kill and eat" (Acts 10:13 NIV), Peter's response is far from enthusiastic. Can't you just see the shocked and appalled look on his face when he responds with, "Surely not, Lord, I have never eaten anything impure or unclean" (Acts 10:14 NIV). In the next verse, God replies, "Do not call anything impure that God has made clean" (Acts 10:15 NIV). According to the Bible, how many times does this same interaction occur between Peter and God?

_____

I don't know about you, but I'm getting the sense that God is pretty serious about ensuring that Peter takes this to heart. Talk about shocking and revolutionary news that turns your world upside down. Peter has to come to terms with the fact that God's salvation, the good news he is giving his life to spread, is not just for the Jews but for *everyone,* Gentiles included. For generations, prejudice was assembled against these "unclean people." Now, God's holy and consecrated people—His chosen people— are to sit side by side at the Great Banquet, sharing a meal with none other than them (Luke 14:15–23).

I wonder if this was a hard pill for Peter to swallow. Thankfully, he responded much better than I would have. Only eleven verses later, Peter meets up with Cornelius at his house. With a larger group of his close friends and relatives gathered there, he preaches a compelling message. Read what he says in Acts 10:27–28, 34–43.

In verse 43, Peter says, "All the prophets testify about him that _____ who believes in him receives forgiveness of sins through his name" (NIV).

> **Let us look to Ephesians:**
>
> All praise to God, the Father of our Lord Jesus Christ, who has blessed us with every spiritual blessing in the heavenly realms because we are united with Christ. Even before he made the world, God loved us and chose us in Christ to be holy and without fault in his eyes. God decided in advance to adopt us into his own family by bringing us to himself through Jesus Christ. This is what he wanted to do, and it gave him great pleasure. So we praise God for the glorious grace he has poured out on us who belong to his dear Son. He is so rich in kindness and grace that he purchased our freedom with the blood of his Son and forgave our sins. He has showered his kindness on us, along with all wisdom and understanding.
>
> God has now revealed to us his mysterious plan regarding Christ, a plan to fulfill his own good pleasure. And this is the plan: At the right time he will bring everything together under the authority of Christ—everything in heaven and on earth (Ephesians 1:3–10 NLT).

According to this passage, what is the "mystery of His will" that is made known to you?

_____

_____

_____

I, for one, am thankful for people like Peter, Paul (the author of Ephesians), and Matthew, who listened to God and began taking Jesus's message of forgiveness, love, and grace, not just to the Jews, but to the Gentiles, too. I am thankful that women like Tamar, Rahab, Ruth, and Bathsheba made their way into Jesus's genealogy. Not just because I see myself in them, for I am Gentile, scarred, and unclean, but more because of what this says about God. The story He is telling doesn't only involve a select group of people who just happen to be born to the right parents in the right part of the world. The story He is telling comes with an open invitation, an invitation outlined for us in Ephesians 2, which we read in closing yesterday. The bottom line is that *anyone* can participate and *everyone* is welcome. It's the story of a God who chooses broken people to pick up the broken pieces of a world that is desperately hurting, so they can join Him in the redemptive work of putting it all back together. Praise the Lord for that!

Before we finish for today, let's ask ourselves one very important question. Is there any one person (this might be a family member, someone from work, a neighbor) that drives you crazy? This person may get under your skin in ways you cannot even begin to describe. How would your interactions with this person change if you began to see them as God does? Are you willing to come face-to-face with your prejudices and allow God to change your perspective as He did for Peter?

Let's pray. Would you join with me in thanking Him for being a God who is all-inclusive and whose open arms are always outstretched for anyone who would come to Him?

> *Thank You, Jesus, for choosing us, all of us, to join with You in the work You are doing to bring healing, wholeness, grace, and peace to a world that is broken. Teach me about my role. Teach me how to listen and respond to Your Spirit. Teach me to see people through Your eyes. Make me more like You.*

Day Four

FIRM FOUNDATION

But whatever were gains to me I now consider loss for the sake of Christ (Philippians 3:7 NIV).

We spent the last three days acquainting ourselves with Jesus's genealogy. I hope that grasping Matthew's reasons and overall purpose for beginning with this list of names has been as enlightening for you as it was for me. For the remainder of our weeks together, we will be focusing on how the lives of these five women intersected with God, ultimately landing them in Matthew's first chapter. Before we get there, I'd like to do a exercise which I am hoping will give a more personal context and shed light on our individual journeys. Undoubtedly, the genealogy of Jesus provides the necessary beginning for our further examination of these women's lives, but this study is not just about these women and how their stories became intertwined with God's story. It is also about how our lives have been wrapped and folded into that very same story. For the next two days, we will examine and study our own genealogies and see how God is entwined in and writing our stories, too.

I understand that for some of you digging up the past might unearth old hurts and reopen wounds you would much rather leave alone. It is not my intention to cause you pain or heartache. However, there is something especially fascinating about studying where we have come from and the family members who preceded us. A peek into the past certainly holds within it the possibility of allowing us greater insight into our own unique personalities and, perhaps, even our struggles.

The subject of history is taught in every elementary, middle, and high school around the world. My son's kindergarten class had the opportunity to raid and pillage the school, taking certain students captive, as a sort of living and breathing lesson accompanying their Viking unit. Upon his arrival home, he proudly announced that he had plucked his older brother right out of his first grade classroom and made him march around their school. Why do we find it necessary for our children to learn about such horrors as Vikings, the Civil War, and the Holocaust? Is it really important to expose them to the extreme measures evil humanity has been capable of over the years? The answer is yes. Not only *were* we capable of all kinds of heinous acts, we still are. The eighteenth century British statesman, Edmund Burke, said, "Those who don't know history are destined to repeat it." Knowledge is power, especially when it comes to this particular application.

Not only does the collective history of mankind influence our lives today, but our personal histories wield a certain amount of power over our present lives as well. Although our history does not have to define us, it will, unless we choose to allow it to refine us instead. This concept, is one we find in Scriptures as well. "For you know that God paid a ransom to save you from the empty life you inherited from your ancestors. And it was not paid with mere gold or silver, which lose their value. It was the precious blood of Christ, the sinless, spotless Lamb of God (1 Peter 1:18–19 NLT).

Who was it that handed down to us the "empty way of life?"

_____

_____

In *Young's Literal Translation,* this phrase you just wrote is, "delivered by fathers." The Greek word is *patroparadotos* and means something that is passed from one's forefathers. This is ultimately the life lessons, information, teachings, and practices that are passed down from one generation to the next.

This verse, of course, implies that there are certain customs, habits, and instructions that may not be beneficial, but might cause us harm. If you are reading this and you are a mother, then I can almost guarantee that you have experienced moments, in which you said or did something that you know came as a direct result of the way your mother did or said something to you. Without even thinking, purely out of habit, you imitate what you saw put into practice. Sometimes this is a wonderful and healthy thing. Sometimes, as Peter is pointing out, we have to come to terms with the fact that what was handed down to us was an empty way of life. A path that seems good, right, and natural to us, can lead to a dead end at times. It reminds me of a gerbil running as fast as its little legs will allow on one of those exercise wheels, believing that if it just keeps moving it will end up where it wants to be. I'm not exactly sure what kind of hopes and dreams a gerbil has, but I'm guessing they involve life outside a cage.

Have you ever had this experience? Can you identify with the gerbil, feeling as though you are running and working very hard, but not actually getting anywhere?

_____

_____

For some of us, what is passed down from previous generations is an empty life. Sometimes, though, we are given every ounce of love, wisdom, and truth that our dear parents or grandparents had to squeeze out. They sacrificed their lives in an act of true love that only, as adults, do we begin to understand with some level of clarity and appreciation. I'd like to tell you my story. I come from a rich heritage of committed Jesus followers. The first time a road is carved through mountainous and rocky terrain, it is exceptionally difficult and quite dangerous. My parents, grandparents, and great-grand parents were the ones who forged a road through what might have seemed like an impossibly difficult landscape. And now, I, who choose that same path, can walk with ease and contented security.

Paul had this experience to a certain extent:

> Watch out for those dogs, those evildoers, those mutilators of the flesh. For it is we who are the circumcision, we who serve God by his Spirit, who boast in Christ Jesus, and who put no confidence in the flesh—though I myself have reasons for such confidence.
>
> If someone else thinks they have reasons to put confidence in the flesh, I have more: circumcised on the eighth day, of the people of Israel, of the tribe of Benjamin, a Hebrew of Hebrews; in regard to the law, a Pharisee; as for zeal, persecuting the church; as for righteousness based on the law, faultless (Philippians 3:2–6 NLT).

Write a few of the reasons that Paul felt he could have "confidence in the flesh."

_____

_____

_____

_____

_____

If you were to rank someone by their "level of Jewishness" with one being the least Jewish and ten being the most, Paul was an eleven. He had every reason to boast; in our day and age, you might say he had his life together. But he writes something quite peculiar and interesting in verse 7.

Do not miss this. Fill in the following blanks from that verse:

"I once thought these things were _____, but now I consider them _____ because of what Christ has done" (Philippians 3:7 NLT).

His reasons for confidence in the flesh, which read much like a rather impressive résumé, meant nothing, and mattered little, in comparison to knowing Jesus. He went on to say, "Yes, everything else is worthless when compared with the infinite value of knowing Christ Jesus my Lord. For his sake I have discarded everything else, counting it all as garbage, so that I could gain Christ" (Philippians 3:8 NLT).

The generations before me laid an incredible foundation. They stirred that concrete up with all kinds of joy, peace, love, gentleness, patience, self-control, and faithfulness, making for some solid ground. This concept of a solid foundation is found in Ephesians 2. Read the passage below looking for the word *foundation*.

> So now you Gentiles are no longer strangers and foreigners. You are citizens along with all of God's holy people. You are members of God's family. Together, we are his house, built on the foundation of the apostles and the prophets. And the cornerstone is Christ Jesus himself. We are carefully joined together in him, becoming a holy temple for the Lord. Through him you Gentiles are also being made part of this dwelling where God lives by his Spirit (Ephesians 2: 19–22 NIV).

Who is the chief cornerstone?

_____

_____

If you miss Jesus, you miss everything. Whether your forefathers and foremothers have led you to a well paved road or one with all sorts of gravel and potholes is irrelevant. The only One who will continue to lead you to the true way is Jesus. In John 14:6, Jesus says, "I am the way the truth and the life…" (NIV). I'm not sure He could have put it any more clearly.

As we close today's lesson, let's turn back to 1 Peter 1:18 and keep reading through verse 21. Isn't this the best news that you've ever heard? Before the creation of the world, Christ was chosen to redeem us from the empty way of life passed down to us, not with perishable things like silver or gold, but with his very blood. We need not place our trust in those that came before us, but in the only One who can give us what we truly need. That is, firm footholds on the way that leads to hope. We will always be disappointed by our human inheritance, but the inheritance that comes from God through Jesus is a hope that is guaranteed to never disappoint (Romans 5:5).

You may have read today's lesson and feel as though you are still living like that gerbil we mentioned earlier. Perhaps, there is an emptiness, a void within you that you cannot seem to fill or quench, or a hope you are desperate to find. Perhaps, in this moment you are realizing that you need Jesus more than anything. If this is the case, tell Him that. If you don't know how to pray, that's okay. There is no need for eloquence and there are no right or wrong words. Just invite Him into your story. And if you do this, find one of your Bible study leaders, or someone you trust, and tell them you did. It might feel uncomfortable. You might feel intimidated. You might feel alone. But, you, sister, have just made the best decision you'll ever make. In addition, as you read this, know that I have prayed for you. Know that these words were given to me to write down so that you might come to know God, the One who loved you so much He laid down His life so that you might find yours.

Day Five

KEEPING ACCOUNT

…Christ Jesus himself as the chief cornerstone. In him the whole building is joined together and rises to become a holy temple in the Lord. And in him you too are being built together to become a dwelling in which God lives by his Spirit (Ephesians 2:20–22 NIV).

With yesterday's study in mind and Christ firmly set as your solid foundation, let's turn our attention solely and fully to your individual genealogy. Draw a family tree of sorts, tracing as far back as you like, but if possible, at least to your great-grand parents. If you are blessed to have parents and or grandparents that still walk this earth, then sometime in the next few days pick up the phone and call them. They will be overjoyed to hear your voice on the other end of the line and, I suspect, more than happy to help you with this exercise. It seems to me, that age only increases the hunger for greater knowledge about origins and personal histories. This is a topic that intrigues and captures us more and more as we get older. Some of you may know very little about your history. Perhaps it has been lost with time. Possibly, you have been adopted and your biological information remains unknown. Just do the best you can with whatever constraints and challenges you have. Anything you can unearth might prove interesting and enlightening. I've done this too.

On the next page, I have included a diagram for you to fill out. Here are some steps I would encourage you to follow.

1) To start, write your name in the circle indicated and move up from there, filling in your parents', grand parents', and great-grand parents' names.

2) If the information is available to you, write their birthplaces next to their circle.

3) If the information is available, write the occupation of each family member next to his or her name and birthplace.

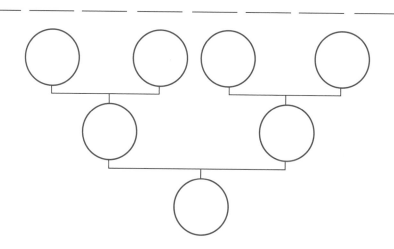

Because this family tree is specifically focused on parents, grandparents, etc., there are not specific ovals for siblings. However, if you have this information, go ahead and write those names in, too.

I have also included some questions below that may help prompt your loved ones recall any illustrations or stories that might assist you. Feel free to detour from these as much or as little as you desire.

1) What is your least favorite childhood memory? What is your best childhood memory?

2) What is the greatest challenge you have ever faced in your life and how did you overcome it?

3) What were some of the most memorable traditions passed down to you from your parents?

4) If you had to sum up each of your parents and grandparents with three words what would they be?

5) If you had to choose one thing that each of your parents and grandparents taught you, which continues to resonate deeply, what would that be?

_____

_____

_____

_____

I hope that you have found this exercise enlightening and that you now possess some newfound knowledge about your personal history and genealogy. I know doing this exercise was an eye-opening experience for me. As I shared in yesterday's lesson, I come from a long line of committed Jesus followers, but studying the lives of my grandparents has made me aware of just how prominent the hand of God has been in my family history. As I did my own homework, my dad reminded me that my grandfather had written a journal about his life, beginning with his early years right up until fairly recently. My grandpa grew up on a farm in western Ukraine and describes his early childhood as mostly enjoyable. He wrote, "My parents were better off than many of their neighbors, and so we lived what we thought was a fairly good life."

He grew up attending church and watched as both his mother and father poured their lives into the local community. His father preached on Sunday mornings, taught Sunday school, and became a head deacon in his church at the age of twenty-five. His mother played guitar and sang in the church choir. They were both highly involved and committed to their local body of believers. This way of life left a lasting impression on my grandfather.

It was not always easy for my grandpa and his family. Living in eastern Europe during the time of the Hitler and Stalin occupations was difficult and trying. There is one moment in particular that, had it gone any way other than it did, would have altered our family tree indefinitely, and not for the better. My uncle has written an especially poignant account of this event, recording it as it was relayed to him. It is an incredibly powerful story, and so, with his permission, I share it with you. I realize I have asked you to give a great deal of your time to today's lesson, but if you are willing to give a few more minutes, I don't think you will be disappointed Please read my uncle's brief narrative.

"The Desperate Journey"
by Marc Sardachuk in memory of Oma (Hulda) Sardachuk

It was January 20th, 1945 and the Russians were quickly pushing the German Army back across the Polish frontier toward Germany. Fleeing with the retreating German forces were waves of refugees: Poles, Ukrainians, and German civilians, all trying to escape from the advancing Soviet army.

These were confusing and chaotic days. Some saw the pursuing Russians as Liberators, ridding Eastern Europe of the terrible Nazi scourge. Others felt that all that was happening was that two tyrants, Hitler and Stalin, were trading places. They knew that the Russians were merciless and vengeful, having already heard the horror stories of reprisals and mistreatment of newly liberated civilians, particularly those who might be accused of having any connection whatsoever with the Germans.

And Hulda knew this too. She firmly believed that being overtaken by the Russians would mean the end for her and her four children, either quickly, by way of execution, or slowly, in the labor camps of Siberia. After all, she was a German citizen alone with her family while her Ukrainian husband was serving in the German army after having been forcibly conscripted eight months earlier. Here she was, trapped with countless other refugees in the main square of a town called Sheroda in western Poland. It was cold, even for January; she was bone tired and she could plainly see that time and hope were running out. Her three daughters, her son, her mother, and sister all looked to her for an answer to their plight but she had none to give them.

It was only three days earlier that they had learned that the Russian capture of their community at Ladorudzek was imminent and they rushed to load their wagon and try to escape by fleeing west to the German/Polish border. She remembered driving her team of horses for two days and nights without sleep. When they did finally stop to rest, she was so exhausted she fell into such a deep sleep that her children could only wake her by slapping and shaking her violently. The journey had almost claimed her son as he nearly froze while sleeping atop the pile of belongings in the back of their wagon. Gun and artillery fire echoed around them as a constant reminder that the war was about as close as the frigid air that filled their lungs. As the hours went by, they plodded along the slippery back roads toward Sheroda and the sounds of the fighting seemed closer with each passing mile. Hulda gripped the reigns of her struggling team and was able to hold her composure only by praying … praying for strength and for deliverance from this terrible situation.

After three long days of struggling on the cold treacherous road, they reached Sheroda and were drawn to the large square in the center of town along with hundreds of other refugee-filled wagons and a large contingent of German army trucks, all clamoring to get to the river. Then they could cross the ice bridge into the city of Poznan and beyond, with the hope of getting to a train bound for Berlin. But as Hulda waited with her family, she knew that time had run out!

The Russians were so close that there was absolutely no hope that a horse-drawn wagon could ever outrun them. The gravity of their situation rested on her shoulders like the weight of the entire world. Hulda gathered her children around her, looked sadly into their eyes and said the words that she had desperately hoped she would never have to say. "Pray, my children, and prepare yourselves to die," she whispered as she closed her own eyes in prayer. Everything was in God's hands; it had been all along, but now nothing short of a miracle could save them. Acceptance of the inevitable must have brought a measure of relief, a complete trust and surrender to the will of God.

Hulda's son, only fourteen, prayed that he would someday see his father again. The eldest daughter, Leonida, continued to hold onto some hope. She was listening to a woman plead in vain with the German driver of a truck that was parked beside their wagon. "Please," cried the woman, "let me ride in the back." The driver simply said "No" and the woman sadly turned and left. But Leonida thought for a moment and then waited. Summoning all of the courage she could muster she walked up to the same truck and driver to plead her case. She addressed the driver and said, "We have a pig that we've slaughtered and we'll give you all the meat if you take us along with you." She looked up at the man, expecting the same answer that he had given the other woman, but to her amazement he said gruffly, "OK, you can ride along." Leonida could hardly contain herself as she spread the news to the rest of the family. The driver did a double take as seven frozen refugees grabbed only what they could carry from their wagon and piled into the back of his truck. *What had he been talked into,* he thought! Oh well, at least he'd have some fresh pork to go with his army rations.

A little while later, as the truck pulled away from the square and headed for the river, Hulda's family was safely stowed with her in the back. She breathed a sigh of relief, folded her hands in her lap, and whispered a prayer of thanksgiving. Even if God had spared them for only one more day, she knew that she would spend what time she had praising Him! And God did spare them, all of them, and He continued to bless Hulda well into her 99th year.

That's a story about my great-grandmother, Hulda Sardachuk. I believe that it was her courage and her faith that shaped much of our destiny as a family. I did not know my Oma well. I was lucky enough to have the opportunity to interact with her on several occasions, which is more than most can say of their relationship with their great-grandmother, I don't remember our conversations well. She spoke with a German accent that was a bit challenging for my young ears. However, I truly believe if I were, through some miraculous sort of time travel, able to sit my thirty-one-year-old self across the table from her thirty-one-year-old self, we would be fast friends.

I believe that her story is parallel to mine. Sure, we lived in very different times and in two very different countries, but, in many ways, we are the same. God saved her that day. No question about it. His hand was upon her and she was spared. Spared from what exactly? Thankfully, we will never know this side of heaven. I'm sure she and God have had more than one conversation about this since her arrival in His presence.

I can identify, because I have been spared also. Not from Russian occupation, but from the rule of other equally damaging forces. I asked Jesus into my heart in a bathroom at church camp, in the fifth grade, with very little understanding of what that meant. But, since that moment, His hand has protected me in more ways than I will ever understand. In my teenage years, He helped me dodge the bullets of peer pressure, sexual temptation, and skewed body image, to name a few. I walked into my college years relatively unscathed. That same hand, that kept me from harm then, has gently moved me, as an adult, towards not just a good life, but an abundant one. A life teeming with blessings and overflowing with His love and grace. I believe that the fruit I am reaping now, in my personal life, in my family life, and in my ministries, is directly tied to God's hand of protection and leading. Like a farmer who carefully and meticulously cares for his crops so that in due time a harvest might be reaped, God's meticulous care of me has led to a harvest of joy and peace I never knew possible. Just like my great-grandmother, I will never know all the ways God has saved me from a path that could have led to disaster, but someday, I trust He'll fill me in. I'm not saying my life is perfect. I'm not saying I have it all together, but I know my life has always been marked by His hand. In Peter's words, "So be content with who you are and don't put on airs. God's strong hand is on you…Live carefree before God, He is the most careful with you" (1 Peter 5:6 MSG).

As we conclude this week, pause for a moment, and reflect on the a few questions. Can you draw any connections between the lives of the family that preceded you and your life today? Have those connections and ties produced good or bad fruit in your life?

If your answer was good fruit, how can you plant seeds and tend the crops to ensure plentiful harvest for future generations? If the answer was bad fruit, how might God be calling you to unchartered land? Land in which, you may be used by God, to create fertile ground, rich soil for the planting of new seeds?

_____

_____

_____

_____

Video Session Two
BEGAT VS. OF

SUBTEXT: HOW ONE WORD CAN CHANGE EVERYTHING!

Begat: to _____ or generate (offspring).

Of: used to indicate possession, _____ , or association.

GALATIANS 4:6-7

We are *all* _____ .

How can we know, that we know, that we know, that we are adopted as outlined by Paul in his letter to the church at Galatia?

1) _____ .

2) We have to _____ that gift, not just with our heads, but our hearts.

Galatians 4:6–7 reveals that through the Spirit of the Son which dwells within us and the relationship and connection the Father shares with Son we have _____ , as well.

MARK 14: 32-36

As Jesus prayed in the garden, He experienced one of His greatest moments of anguish, apart from the cross itself. He said to Peter, James, and John, "My soul is overwhelmed with sorrow to the point of death" (Mark 14:34 NIV). Going a little further, Jesus falls to the ground and prays addressing God as_____ _____ .

Jesus understood that even though He felt completely and utterly alone He is still _____ connected to the Father.

What does this mean for me?

_____

_____

_____

_____

_____

_____

Week Two

PERIPETEIA: TAMAR

[per-*uh*-pi-tahy-*uh*, -tee-*uh*]

noun

1.
a sudden turn of events or an unexpected
reversal, especially in a literary work.

Day One

LITMUS TEST

But you are a chosen people, a royal priesthood, a holy nation, God's special possession, that you may declare the praises of him who called you out of darkness into his wonderful light (1 Peter 2:9 NIV).

This week marks the beginning of our focus on the women from the genealogy of Jesus. I am excited about studying these women with you over the next five weeks. I believe, with my whole heart, that they, although living in a much different time than our own, have much to teach us. We will discover countless ways that their victories and struggles mirror our own.

Having said that, let's begin with the very first woman our eyes meet on the page of Matthew 1, a woman by the name of Tamar. Let's familiarize ourselves with her somewhat obscure story found in Genesis 38 and take a moment to glance over both Genesis 37 and Genesis 39 to get the context for her story. There is no need to read all of chapters 37 and 39; just take a look at some of the headings to learn how this story fits into the overall narrative of Genesis. Of course, if you want to read these chapters, go right ahead.

Briefly summarize chapter 37 below. Who are the main characters?

_____

_____

Briefly summarize what happens in chapter 39. Who are the main characters there?

_____

_____

I realize that those two chapters may not seem like they connect to Tamar, and so, I thank you for being diligent and taking the time to skim through them. We will come back to their significance later. Now, please take a moment to read through Genesis 38 in its entirety.

Sometimes it can be hard to slog through Scripture. I can remember the summer I turned ten. I attended a Christian sports camp just outside of Toronto, where I was living with my parents at the time. I came home with a newly acquired passion to read the Bible. I asked my mom, ever so enthusiastically, "Can you get me a Bible? I really want to read the whole thing." Looking back now, I'm sure she held in some laughter at my naive eagerness, but she conceded and bought me one anyway. After all, it's hard to argue with your daughter when the book she desperately wants is the Bible. I sat down and started voraciously reading, starting the only place I knew to start: the beginning. God made the light, darkness, stars, moon, and animals. "Good, I've got it," I thought. Then He made the people. That was all great stuff, too. My eagerness came to a screeching halt, when I reached Leviticus. I remember thinking, "I'm done now." Sometimes, I confess, I still feel that way, but Genesis 38 reads a lot more like a soap opera. It's high drama, very juicy, and quite scandalous. Try to imagine the story playing out with your favorite actresses and actors, and I bet you won't be able to put your Bible down.

Can you believe this story is in the Bible? I had a hard time believing it myself. Once you've gotten over the shock of it all, glance back to the beginning and reread the first six verses.

Genesis 38:1 says, "Judah went down from his brothers" (ESV). Having glanced through the previous chapter of Genesis, who is Judah's father, and who is his most famous brother?

_____

_____

That's right, Judah was one of Jacob's sons and a brother to Joseph, the man whose story fills the greater part of the last portion of Genesis.

Fill in the following blank from Genesis 1:38. "At that time, Judah _____ his brothers and went down to stay with a man of Adullam named Hirah." (NIV).

When I first read that Judah departed from his brothers, I thought, "Good for him; he's going off on his own adventure, forging his own path." But then, I remembered that for the Jews, leaving your family was not always viewed as a good thing. Back when Moses led the Israelites out of Egypt, out of slavery, and into the desert, God had a very important conversation with Moses on Mount Sinai. This discussion between God and Moses is recorded in Exodus 19. Read Exodus 19:3–6 and summarize it below.

_____

_____

Just to make sure we don't miss what's happening here, fill in the following blank:

"Now if you obey me fully and keep my covenant, then out of all nations you will be my_____ _____ . Although the whole earth is mine, you will be for me a kingdom of _____and a _____nation'…" (Exodus 19:5–6a NIV).

> The role of a priest in ancient Israel was to be a mediator, a middleman between God and His people. One commentator put it this way, "The priest serves as a conduit to bring down God's radiant blessing and influence into this world."
>
> In other words, the "priests represented God to the people, and they represented the people to God."
>
> So, when God says to Moses at Mount Sinai that the Israelites will be a kingdom of priests, He is saying that if anyone has a question as to what God is like, His character, or His daily activities, they simply needed to look

to the character and day-to-day operations of the Israelites and they would find their answer. The Israelites were, in a sense, a living and breathing litmus test. In chemistry, litmus paper can be dipped into a solution to determine the liquid's level of acidity or alkalinity. In that same way, if a person wants to determine whether God is loving or not, they simply needed to examine the actions of the Israelites and make their determination accordingly. No pressure, right? Yikes! If I were Moses receiving that news, I would have immediately broken out in a cold sweat and likely had an anxiety attack on the spot.

You can see why it was important for the Israelites to stay together. Perhaps this is why we find so many laws and statutes recorded in books like Leviticus, Numbers, and Deuteronomy. Read Leviticus 20:7. What does the beginning of the verse tell the Israelites to do?

_____

You got it. Consecrate yourselves. In other words, separate yourselves. *Strong's Bible Dictionary* defines it like this, "to keep oneself separate or apart." We have all heard the phrase, "there is power in numbers." The Israelites probably took that very seriously. If they were going to live set apart, then they needed to be pretty determined to stick together. Let's go back to Genesis 38. When Judah leaves his brothers and goes to stay with Hirah (by the way, Hirah is living in Canaan, which we learned last week means he is a Gentile), it's a big deal. This is neither living "set apart," nor "sticking together."

In 1 Peter "But you are not like that, for you are a chosen people. You are royal priests, a holy nation, God's very own possession. As a result, you can show others the goodness of God, for he called you out of the darkness into his wonderful light" (1 Peter 2:9 NLT).

Who is the "you" Peter is writing about?

_____

That's right. No longer is it only the Israelites who are a "royal priesthood," but all of us who call ourselves followers of Jesus. We now possess the great responsibility of living in a way that points others towards God. We are the litmus test of today. Thankfully, we have something that the Israelites did not have. We have the Holy Spirit with us to be our Helper and to guide us as we aim to live our lives "set apart." However, just as it was then, it is now—we must "stick together."

John says, "I am praying not only for these disciples but also for all who will ever believe in me through their message. I pray that they will all be one, just as you and I are one—as you are in me, Father, and I am in you. And may they be in us so that the world will believe you sent me" (John 17:20–21 NLT). In these verses, who is Jesus praying for?

_____

Why is it so important that all the believers be "one"?

_____

This explicitly points out that if the world is to believe, we must be one with each other, just as Christ is one with the Father. It makes me wonder how Genesis 38 might have read if Judah had just stayed with his family, as he was supposed to do. Instead, he went off on his own and "turned aside to a certain Adullamite" (Genesis 38:1 ESV). As we conclude today's lesson, let's have a moment of personal reflection. Have you witnessed, in either your life, or someone else's, a "turning aside," to quote the words of Genesis 38:1, that ultimately had negative consequences? Or have you seen the benefits of choosing to stay connected to a group of believers (blood family or family in Christ)?

Are there any obstacles that stand in the way of you and your fellow believers from being "one?" If so, what steps do you need to take to work towards reconciliation? Remember, those on the outside are watching. How we treat one another is often the litmus test for their acceptance or denial of God. There's a lot at stake—often more than we know. Let's make it our goal , as Paul wrote, to be "like-minded, having the same love, being one in spirit and of one mind" (Philippians 2:2b NIV).

Day Two

CLEARING THE AIR

For my yoke is easy and my burden is light (Matthew 11:30 NIV).

Let's start today with just a brief recap of what is happening in our story so far. Judah, brother of Joseph, has left his family and gone to stay with a friend named Hirah. Judah meets a woman, the daughter of a Canaanite man named Shua, marries her, and then has three sons, Er, Onan, and Shelah, with her. Genesis 24:3 says, "… and I will make you swear by the Lord, the God of heaven and the God of the earth, that you will not take a wife for my son from the daughters of the Canaanites, among whom I dwell…" (NIV). This verse is straight to the point instructing Judah not to marry a Canaanite woman, and yet, Judah marries the first woman that catches his eye regardless of the fact that his God has specifically told him not to. Once his sons are of age, Judah chooses a wife for his firstborn, Er, and the name of this woman is Tamar.

Let's pick up with the text. Read Genesis 38:7–10. Are you feeling a bit unnerved by everything you just read? I have to admit, I was, when I first read these verses. Being as forthright as you can, what is your initial reaction to the following text: "But Er, Judah's firstborn, was wicked in the sight of the Lord, and the Lord put him to death" (Genesis 38:7 ESV).

Not exactly settling is it? We aren't told the details of Er's sin, which ultimately resulted in his death. But several commentaries compare the phrase "wicked in the sight of the Lord" found in Genesis 38:7 to the phrase, "Now the men of Sodom were wicked exceedingly" found in Genesis 13:13. Sodom was a city that was synonymous with sexual immorality, so it may be that Er's sin was sexual in nature. Another commentary points out that it is entirely possible that God did not put him to death by "direct visitation" but instead may have allowed Er to "reap the first fruits of his youthful indulgence.

Don't we all know that sometimes the consequences that come as a result of a sin are much worse than the sin itself? In any event, let's move to the heart of the lesson which lands us in verses 8–9. Verse 8 highlights an Israelite law and custom found in Deuteronomy 25:5–10. What does this law state?

_____

_____

This may seem strange in today's culture. I can't imagine any widow nowadays that would go for the idea of marrying her brother-in-law. However, I did attend a dear friend's wedding in which the groom's brother was the best man. As is customary in today's weddings, the best man gave a speech or toast to the bride and groom. In his speech, he cited this law: the custom of Levirate marriage, promising that if a tragedy were to befall his brother, he would be more than happy to marry his sister-in-law. Since the groom and his brother were both pastor's kids and the room was full of life-long churchgoers, the wedding attendees erupted with laughter.

Why did they have a law like this back then? The purpose of the custom of Levirate marriage was twofold:

1) It allowed the name of the brother to be carried on, the family line continued, and the land rightfully distributed to the family through a legal heir.

2) It protected the widow, giving her children to support her and the ability to avoid living the rest of her life as a destitute woman.

> Have you ever wondered why a rule exists? I'm sure all of us can think back to our teenage years and easily remember a time our parents enforced a rule that felt unfair or unfounded. Perhaps you even said something like, "Why are you trying to ruin my life? Or maybe this hits a little too close to home right now as you are attempting to navigate the treacherous road of raising a preadolescent or adolescent. My husband, Michael, taught middle

school Bible for five years, prior to becoming a pastor at our church, and spent many a lesson explaining why it might be that his students' parents had certain rules established in their homes. He often reassured them that it was highly unlikely that their parents hated them. You might laugh, but I bet if we were honest with ourselves, there were times that our parents' rules, or maybe even God's, have felt burdensome to us.

Let's take a look at some of God's most famous rules. Turn to Exodus 20:1–17 and fill in the chart below. In the left hand column write the rule (you can abbreviate it) and on the right, briefly record why you think that rule might have been established by God.

	Rule	Why God Established
1		
2		
3		
4		
5		
6		
7		
8		
9		
10		

I hope you have observed the pattern emerging from this exercise. Every rule God puts into place is for our good. Why would He say, "Have no other gods before me" (Exodus 20:3 ESV)? Maybe because He knew we would have a tendency to believe all sorts of things might bring worth, value, and meaning to our lives. Maybe He knew we would try to find our identity in our jobs, money, a nice house, or a spouse—all things that would leave us feeling empty in the end. Why would He say, "You shall not misuse the name of the Lord your God" (Exodus 20:7 NIV)? Maybe because He knew that all sorts of people would attribute their own agendas, even their plans for revenge, to God's calling on their lives, leading to all kinds of atrocities—genocide, slavery, and war upon war in His name. Why would He say, "Remember the Sabbath" (Exodus 20:8 NIV)? Maybe because He knew how we all have a tendency to drive ourselves into the ground, believing that our ultimate significance would come from what we did, as opposed to who we are in Christ. And why would He put something like the custom of Levirate marriage into place? Maybe because He understood that women living in that time had absolutely no rights and no value apart from their connection to the men in their lives—their fathers and husbands. He knew the kind of harm woman were vulnerable to if they were left alone with no one to defend and support them.

God cares about us. Just like a mother calmly directing her unstable one-year-old toddler away from a flight of stairs. Or a Father, gently—or not so gently—urging his son, armed with a learner's permit, to brake a little earlier and avoid collision with the car in front of him. We, as parents, only want what is best for our children. We have rules in our homes to protect our kids from physical danger or the more terrifying and seemingly unpredictable, emotional or spiritual danger. The same is true of God, *our* heavenly Father. Read Matthew 11:28–30. What do you think Jesus meant by these words?

_____

I have encountered many people who have come from a church tradition that is stifling—one that is heavy on rules and light on grace. They have grown up believing that if they didn't follow certain rules—if they fell short in any way—that they were somehow condemned for life. I have a dear friend, who chose not to have her son baptized in the Catholic Church as a baby. She was told by her Catholic Grandma that her sweet baby boy would certainly endure hell if tragedy befell. My friend was distraught.

Can you relate to my friend's experience? If so, explain.

_____

_____

_____

_____

Perhaps this is why Jesus says, "For my yoke is easy and my burden is light" (Matthew 11:30 NIV). He did not come to "condemn the world, but to save the world through Him" (John 3:17b NIV). Following the rules, or I suppose I'd rather say adhering to the boundaries God has placed, only makes our lives easier. They bring life, not death. Within God's boundaries, there is rest for our souls, not the heavy burden of judgment. Let's close by reflecting on Romans 8:1–2.

> With the arrival of Jesus, the Messiah, that fateful dilemma is resolved. Those who enter into Christ's being-here-for-us no longer have to live under a continuous, low-lying black cloud. A new power is in operation. The Spirit of life in Christ, like a strong wind, has magnificently cleared the air, freeing you from a fated lifetime of brutal tyranny at the hands of sin and death (MSG).

Thank You, Jesus, for clearing the air.

Day Three

IMPOSSIBLE CIRCUMSTANCES

No chance at all if you think you can pull it off yourself. Every chance in the world if you trust God to do it (Matthew 19:26 MSG).

I hope the perspective we gained yesterday helps you to feel less bogged down and shackled by the burden of rules in your life. Have the words of Paul, "There is therefore now no condemnation for those who are in Christ Jesus" (Romans 8:1 ESV), settled into your soul? Today, we continue reading the story of Judah and Tamar. Although I would like to say we are through the most scandalous parts, the truth is, we are only just beginning. Get ready to have your mind blown. You will find yourself amazed, undoubtedly, that certain portions of this text are found within the Holy Scriptures. Read Genesis 38:11–14.

Let me start by saying, I warned you. It gets a little messy, doesn't it? Let's be sure we get a clear picture of what is unfolding. Reread verse 11 and answer the following questions:

What does Judah tell Tamar to do?

_____

_____

What is the reason for Judah's actions?

_____

_____

Did you catch that? The Scripture says, "for he feared that he would die, like his brothers" (Genesis 38:11 ESV). For he what? He *feared*. What he should have done, according to the Levirate law we studied yesterday, was to give Shelah to be married to Tamar, regardless of his reservations and despite his fear. Instead, he sends her back to her father. Metaphorically, he is shoving the whole situation under the rug. I'm sure Judah reasoned that if he just sent her away, the whole mess would go away as well.

I see a scenario similar to this play out in my house frequently. My two middle two sons have a tendency to get on each other's nerves. Wesley will take Crosby's sword. Crosby will respond in anger and hit Wesley in the head with said sword, which will propel them both into tears. It usually results with me leaving what I am doing to come and referee the situation.

Wesley will say something like "Crosby hit me in the head!" Wes has a flare for the dramatic so he is usually writhing around on the ground as if he has just been struck by a real Samurai sword, as opposed the foam sword that actually was responsible for the blow.

Crosby will say, "He took my sword."

When I look to Wesley to confirm whether the whole scene in my living room did begin with a stolen sword, he will quickly say, "I didn't take it!" Fear, anger, shame, and blame.

This pattern of emotions is exactly what is being demonstrated by Judah in our story. We are told that Judah's wife died and once he had grieved, he headed to Timnah. There he joins Hirah (his friend mentioned in the beginning of the chapter) for a festival that includes the shearing of sheep. Although it does not explicitly state in the Scripture, Judah is having a very good time. Just so I know we are on the same page, let me say it even clearer: he's in "high spirits." In fact, he's drunk. What does it say that Tamar did in verses 13–14?

_____

_____

Tamar disguises herself as a temple prostitute and places herself strategically along the roadside, knowing that her father-in-law will be making his way there soon. There are two very important prepositions found in verses 13–14 that clearly indicate that Tamar has purposefully plotted for the events to unfold the way they do. If she were on trial in our modern-day court system, the prosecution would clearly be able to prove criminal intent.

Fill in the following blanks. "And _____ Tamar was told 'Your father-in-law is going up to Timnah to sheer his sheep,' she took off her widow's garments and covered herself with a veil, wrapping herself up, and sat at the entrance to Enaim, which is on the road to Timnah. _____ she saw that Shelah was grown up, and she had not been given to him in marriage" (Genesis 38:13–14 ESV).

The "when" and the "for" give her away. Now, you might be thinking like I did, "Give the girl a break." I mean all she really wants is to be married and start a family. She's been living with her father for who knows how long. Waiting and waiting and waiting for Judah to follow through on his promise. The constant waiting would drive anyone to make rash and questionable choices. Can anyone blame her for her actions? I feel for the poor girl. I really do. If I were in her shoes, maybe I would have done the same thing. Perhaps some of you reading this are single. You don't want to be, but you are. It feels as though everyone around you is getting married or having babies and your life is a revolving door of bridal and baby showers. You're certain the phrase "always a bridesmaid, never a bride" was penned specifically for you. You think that if your friends post any more rants about how challenging and difficult life is as a stay-at-home mom, you might just reach through the computer and strangle someone. You would give your left arm to have children that drove you crazy enough to post rants on social media.

Surely, Tamar is feeling a whole cocktail of emotions including, but not limited to, the following: anger, frustration, betrayal, sadness, grief, confusion, and despair. These emotions are completely warranted. You might even say that Judah has put her in an impossible situation. What is she to do? But it's not her emotions that are unreasonable; they aren't the issue. The cause of the problem is what she does in response to her emotions. Have you ever done something that you knew in your heart was wrong but you felt justified in doing it? Maybe there's a Judah in your life who you feel has forced your hand, and you felt there was no other way to respond than by doing something that came in direct conflict with what your conscience was telling you. Take some time to reflect on this question. If you have a personal experience or know of someone who walked through something similar, record it below.

_____

_____

It's tough, isn't it? It's tough to do the right thing when everything in you feels justified to do the exact opposite. I was a pretty good kid. I tend to be a people pleaser, which means the part of me that doesn't want to disappoint or let others down often governs my choices. However, my mom tells of a time when I was quite young that we were visiting one of her friend's homes. Her friend had a son that was pestering and irritating me and refused to leave me alone. I got so upset that I bit him. Hard. My mom understood that my emotions were justified, but my bottom was on the receiving end of my very first spanking, regardless of how warranted my retaliation seemed to me. There was a point to be made. Even though he deserved it, I had made a wrong choice, one that demanded a response from my mom.

Read the story of the rich, young ruler in Matthew 19:16–30.

At first glance, this story seems to be strictly about money, but read it more carefully. There's a lot more going on. The young ruler comes to Jesus with a question about how he can inherit eternal life. Jesus tells him if he wants to have life to the fullest, to follow the commandments. Don't murder. Don't commit adultery. Love your neighbor as yourself. The young ruler responds by saying, "All these I have kept. What do I still lack?" (Mathew 19:20 ESV). Here's where it gets tricky because Jesus asks him to do something that he isn't expecting. He sees right through him to the root issue—to the one thing that holds this man's heart captive. "Jesus said to him, 'If you would be perfect, go, sell what you possess and give to the poor'" (Matthew 19:21 ESV). In one devastating moment, the man walks away. It wasn't an issue of money. It was an issue of trust. Jesus was ultimately asking him if he was willing to follow Him, even to places that were uncomfortable, even when what He asked seemed impossible? Perhaps that's why when Jesus's disciples asked Him later, "Who then can be saved?" Jesus says, "With man this is impossible, but with God all things are possible" (Matthew 19:26 ESV).

> I like it even better in The Message Translation, "The disciples were staggered, 'Then who has any chance at all?' Jesus looked hard at them and said, 'No chance at all if you think you can pull it off yourself. Every chance in the world if you trust God to do it'" (Matthew 19: 25–26 MSG).

Perhaps Tamar felt this way. Judah had her in an impossible situation. Was there any other way than to take matters into her own hands? Maybe she felt like there was no chance for her otherwise, so she executed a well-constructed plan. What she lacked was trust. Trust that God had her back. Trust that He could work it all out. Trust that even though she couldn't see a way out, God could. I wonder if this hits home for any of you, like it does me. It's so easy to take matters into our own hands and to attempt to pull things off on our own, but how quickly we can make a mess of things. Let's close with a time of reflection. Try to answer these questions as honestly as you possibly can. I am praying for you, my dear sisters. Let God lead you to places you may not want to go. It's not easy, but I promise you, it's worth it.

In what areas of your life do you try to take matters into your own hands the most?

_____

_____

What would it look like to trust God in those areas?

_____

_____

_____

Do you believe that God can do the impossible? Do you think He is worthy of your trust?

_____

_____

_____

Take some time to pray and ask God to help you as you learn to trust Him more.

Day Four

CONFLICT RESOLUTION

If a fellow believer hurts you, go and tell him—work it out between the two of you (Matthew 18:15 MSG).

Today, we will finish Genesis 38. We will spend time tomorrow reflecting on how this story fits into the greater picture painted within the Bible. For now, read Genesis 38:15–30.

We learned yesterday that although Tamar's emotions were understandable, her choice to take matters into her own hands was not a good one. And her plan was intentional, not a haphazard plot. It was calculated, thought out, and shrewdly executed. The art of manipulation is one most women excel in, including me. We know exactly what buttons to push, when, and how to push them to get exactly what we want. We prey on the vulnerabilities of others, especially when it comes to the opposite sex. Is there anyone that hasn't turned on the tears to get out of a ticket or strategically chosen an outfit, or lack thereof, to get their way? There is no denying it; if we are honest, we know just what we are doing. So did Tamar. What three things did she ask for as a pledge for the goat Judah promised her?

_____

_____

_____

These three items probably don't mean much to us nowadays. When was the last time you saw someone walking down the street with a staff? But in Tamar's time, these items were like asking for someone's license and fingerprints. The seal was constructed of metal and stone and was worn around the owner's neck. Like a stamp in today's time, it could be pressed into clay, leaving an impression, which ultimately identified its owner. The staff had markings that pinpointed the owner as well. Tamar knew she would need proof, and asking for Judah's personal items were essential to her plan.

We read that Judah sent his friend Hirah to bring the goat to the "temple prostitute" only to learn that she was nowhere to be found. He then exclaims, "Let her keep the things as her own, or we shall be laughed at" (Genesis 38:23 ESV). A man who sends his friend to do his dirty work and has no reservations about letting his one-of-a-kind personal items go in an attempt to save face is a man well acquainted with his own guilt. And guilt motivates us to do some interesting things.

When Judah learns, three months later, that Tamar is pregnant, what is his response?

_____

_____

He doesn't really mince words here, does he? It's at this point that I want to take Judah by the shoulders and shake some sense into him. I would like to get in real close to his face and scream at the top of my lungs, "What did you expect her to do?" At the heart of his response is a man filled with remorse and shame. He's tried to outrun his conscience, but it's caught up with him. Now, there's no more avoiding it. Shoving the blame on Tamar seemed like the best solution; he thinks it might release him from having to take any real responsibility for the way things had turned out.

Jesus understood our human tendency to respond in the same manner that Judah did when it comes to being on the receiving end of blame. Read Matthew 7:1–5 and summarize the passage below.

_____

_____

Did you see what Jesus is doing here? The visual illustration he uses is almost ridiculous. A speck of sawdust and a wood plank. I'm not sure it would even be possible to see with an enormous plank in your eye. Of course, that's His point. When our own pride and guilt are in the way, our perspective is a little skewed. And when I say a little skewed, I mean a lot. We'll do anything to take the attention off us and shift it to someone else.

Has your guilt and pride ever led you to shift unnecessary blame on others?

_____

_____

This is a tough question. Mostly because, if I'm to answer it honestly, it's an emphatic "Yes!" I have the uncanny ability to make my husband feel as though he is to blame at the end of many arguments. It can begin with something I have done that has caused him frustration, something I am guilty of, and end with an apology, not from me, but from him. Why? Because it is much easier to look at the speck of sawdust in someone else's eye rather than address the unwieldy plank in my own. Am I alone in this, or can you identify?

Before we close today, I want to take a look at Tamar's response. I think it can teach us a great deal, not just about her, but on how we choose to interact with those who have hurt us deeply. Reread verses 25 and fill in the blanks: "As she was _____ _____ out, she _____ _____ to her father-in-law…" (Genesis 28:25 ɛsv).

She makes an interesting choice here. One I'm not sure I would have made had I been in her shoes. She chooses a quiet and respectful confrontation versus a public announcement. The Scripture tells us she is about to be brought out. It doesn't say exactly where but I'm assuming it was going to be a high profile scenario—somewhere heavily populated. I'm picturing *The Scarlet Letter* here. Perhaps, I'm reading too much into this story, but I doubt it. Tamar would have had the opportunity to shout Judah's guilt from the rooftops. He certainly gave her enough fuel to fan the fire, but she doesn't. This, much like the speck and the plank illustration, hits a little too close to home for comfort. When someone wrongs me, I not only want him or her to know it, I want *everyone* to know it. When someone cuts in front of me in line, I mumble under my breath, but loud enough for onlookers to hear. If someone steals the parking spot I was waiting for, I lay on my horn. I want to be sure there's not one person nearby that doesn't catch on to the injustice I feel is being committed. The truth is that is not the way Jesus wants us to live. He wants us to forgive. Now, don't get me wrong here. If someone has mistreated you, lied to you, hurt you, offended you, fill-in-the-blank you, I'm not saying you should just ignore it. Of course, you should not let people walk all over you or abuse you with no response or rebuttal on your part. What I am saying is that there is a right and wise way to address problems, none of which include sharing your whole messy situation with anyone and everyone who will stand still long enough to listen.

> Matthew has some very specific words about how to handle conflict.
>
> If a fellow believer hurts you, go and tell him—work it out between the two of you. If he listens, you've made a friend. If he won't listen, take one or two others along so that the presence of witnesses will keep things honest, and try again. If he still won't listen, tell the church. If he won't listen to the church, you'll have to start over from scratch, confront him with the need for repentance, and offer again God's forgiving love (Matthew 18:15–17 MSG).

In this passage, we get some instructions on how to handle disagreements. Are these instructions directed at a certain group of people? What group is that?

_____

This concept was meant to apply to those within the church. Those who call themselves followers of Jesus, those that would categorize themselves as disciples. If our issue is with someone outside of the church, we simply cannot hold them accountable to the same set of rules and laws by which we govern our lives. This does not mean that we should avoid confrontation entirely, but just that we can't expect the other party involved to respond in the same manner as a fellow believer might or should. When two people who desire to put Jesus first in their lives have conflict between them, there is a third party intrinsically involved. I'm not talking about a witness invited to help with the peacemaking process in the instructions above. I'm talking about the Holy Spirit. When the physical presence of Jesus left earth, he gave us a Friend, as John put it to "make everything plain" (John 14:25 MSG) and to remind us of the things Jesus said while He was living amongst us. Is it fair for us to impose the same standards on those living with that Spirit as to those living without it?

As we finish today's lesson, take some time to think about your interpersonal dealings with others and answer the following question. How do you respond when others hurt or wrong you?

_____

_____

_____

Do you follow the model found in Matthew 18? Or are you guilty of airing out yours and others dirty laundry to anyone who will listen? Do you withdraw, perhaps, hoping your hurts will go away on their own?

_____

_____

How might your dealings with non-believers change after today's lesson?

_____

_____

_____

_____

Day Five

SHAME, BLAME, COVER, HIDE, AND RUN

Today we find ourselves at the end of the story of Tamar. I warned you that it was going to be messy, and I don't think I let you down on my promise. Sometimes it's utterly shocking what's inside the Bible. It's easy to skip over stories like these. We find the story of Judah and Tamar nestled in the middle of the much more glamorous story of Joseph. Judah, the black sheep of the family, and Tamar, the desperate widow who was willing to sell herself to make a point. I lift my head high and turn away in disgust wondering, "How could she be so shameless?" But then, I remember their mess is my mess. We, too, are subject to the same sins that took Judah and Tamar captive because they are the exact sins that enticed Eve in the garden a very long time ago.

Let's go back to the beginning. Read Genesis 3:1 and fill in the blank. "He" refers to the serpent. It states, "He said to the woman, "Did _____, 'You must not eat from any tree in the garden'?" (NIV).

There is a good reason the serpent is called *craftier* than any of the other animals. Look at what he is doing! It's brilliant in its deviousness. The serpent is well aware that if he is going to lead Eve down the path he has set, it all must begin with this one inherently dangerous and deceptively innocent question, "Did God really say…?" (Genesis 3:1 NIV). Take a moment, and speak this questions aloud so it will stick in your head, "Did God really say…?" Does God really love you? Does He really know what's best? Is He really worthy of your trust? Is He even real? If He really cared for you, wouldn't things be different? I wonder how much of our own heartbreak and regret can be traced back to this one single and hauntingly posed question? With this one question, Satan struck a chord of doubt deep in the core of Eve's being. What has doubt done to you?

_____

_____

Tamar doubted that God could lead her out of a seemingly impossible situation. Much like Tamar, my doubts lead me to take matters into my own hands. Our sister, Eve, suffered from the same predisposition. Let's keep reading in Genesis 3. Verse 6 says, "When the woman saw that the fruit of the tree was good for food and pleasing to the eye and also _____ for _____ _____, she took some and ate it" (NIV).

Eve's first mistake was allowing those doubts to creep in and take hold of her. Her next mistake, a very costly one, was to believe that wisdom could be found in a piece of fruit. I imagine that her inner monologue went something like this:

> Did God really say I shouldn't eat from that tree, that special tree in the middle of the garden? Well, I guess He did say that, but why? Why would He tell us that every other tree was okay except for that one? I mean, it has to be because that one is special. That's what the serpent said. If I eat of that fruit then my eyes will be opened and I will be like God. He must have told me not to eat of it because He doesn't want me to be like Him. Well, that seems kind of unfair doesn't it? He told us He would share every good thing with us but that was a lie. That was a lie, because if it were true, He would have let us eat of that special tree. I mean really, what's the worst thing that could happen? There's no way God would cause me to die. That seems way too extreme and besides, if He doesn't have Adam and I, who would walk with Him in the garden? He would be alone. All I really want is to be wiser. Wouldn't God like it if I was wiser? More like Him? I mean, it's just a piece of fruit. What's the big deal anyway?

I wonder if this is what she thought right before she took her first big bite. If only she would have known the pain this would cause. If only she would have understood the cycle of sin that her actions would set into motion.

I get angry with her sometimes when I read this story. I think, "Eve, how could you be so foolish?" Then I realize I'm just like her. I'm just like Tamar. I believe that God does not know what is best for me. I also find it difficult to trust Him. I believe that things would be different—better perhaps—if I took matters into my own hands. Tamar figured she had waited long enough for God to intervene, give her a husband, and save her from her desolate life. She thought she could fix it on her own. I can identify with that sentiment. I, too, have taken the reins right out of God's hands at times. I hope that I can steer the wild and crazy horse that is my life. I believe I can cause it to submit with the sheer force of my will. The problem is that life isn't much like a horse at all. There is no amount of force or human will that can effect a whole lot of change.

Can you see yourself in Eve and Tamar? What kinds of things do you put your hope in, believing they will bring you what you desire, only to be disappointed?

_____

_____

Pride is one word that sums up the rationale behind the choices of Adam and Eve, and the word that most frequently leads us into the same mess they found themselves in. Pride says, "I don't need help." It says, "My way is better." Pride tells us is that everything can be resolved through our own manipulation and control. If we believe that ever-enticing lie, we find ourselves much like Adam and Eve did in the Genesis 3 story. Read Genesis 3:7–13 and answer the following questions:

Why would they make coverings for themselves?

_____

What did they do when they heard the Lord God walking in the garden?

_____

Why did they hide?

_____

What do both Adam and Eve do when confronted by God to give an account for their actions?

_____

_____

_____

> Shame, cover, fear, blame, and hide. These five words pretty much sum it all up. In a moment, the perfect harmony they experienced with their God came apart at the seams. They traded the Creator for the creation. They glanced down to realize for the first time that they were naked, and shame crept into their story. It's their shame that motivated them to reach down and pick up fig leaves, sew them together, and cover themselves. Their shame caused them to fear God and run from Him as opposed to toward Him. Their shame led them to blame. "Surely, it's not my fault," I envision them saying, as they pointed their finger at one another.
>
> Doubt leads to pride and pride is usually followed by these five responses. We see this pattern repeated over and over again throughout the course of history. It's the one that's played out in the story of Tamar. Revisit the following verses and fill in the blank to complete the verse. In the space below each verse, fill in which of the responses is best represented (there may be more than one). Here are the responses again: shame, blame, fear, cover, and hide.

Genesis 38:11: "Then Judah said to Tamar his daughter-in-law, 'Remain a widow in your father's house, until Shelah my son grows up'—for he _____ that he would die…" (ESV).

Genesis 38:4: "she took off her widow's garments and _____ herself with a veil" (ESV).

Genesis 38:24b: "And Judah said, 'Bring her out and let her be burned'" (ESV).

_____.

Shame, blame, fear, cover, and run. No matter how hard we try, it's difficult to get away from these words, isn't it? I can remember when I was a little girl. I closed the car door on my dad's fingers. It was an accident, of course, but the look of pain on his face as a result of something I had done was almost too much to handle. Even though I did not do it on purpose, I couldn't escape the overwhelming sense of shame. The only thing I could think to do was to run and hide in the laundry room closet. It took my parents a while to figure out where I had gone. When they opened the closet doors, there I was, head in my hands, tears streaming down my face—a puddled mess on the floor. I get the sense this is exactly how Adam and Eve felt, huddled behind a tree in the garden that day. I wonder, can any of you recall a time where you felt that way? If so, record it briefly below.

_____

_____

_____

_____

It could be devastating to end on this depressing note. We will spend more time in the video discussing how Jesus changed the trajectory of the story, but, for now, let's meditate on this passage penned by Paul in Romans 5.

> You know the story of how Adam landed us in the dilemma we're in—first sin, then death, and no one is exempt from either sin or death. That sin disturbed relations with God in everything and everyone…But Adam, who got us into this, also points ahead to the One who will get us out of it…Here it is in a nutshell: Just as one person did it wrong and got us in all this trouble with sin and death, another person did it right and got us out

of it. But more than just getting us out of trouble, He got us into life! One man said no to God and put many people in the wrong; one man said yes to God and put many in the right (Romans 5: 12–19 MSG).

Praise be to God that "shame, blame, cover, hide, and run" are not the end of the story. There's a new story that Jesus is writing in our hearts and lives. Thank You, Jesus, for giving us life.

Video Session Three
UNEXPECTED TURNS

HISTORICAL REVIEW

Jacob has _____ sons, which represent the twelve _____ of Israel.

INHERITANCE RIGHTS OF THE FIRSTBORN

1) The firstborn male will take on the _____ roles within the family.

2) The firstborn male will receive a _____ _____ of the inheritance.

REUBEN

Genesis 35:22 says, "While Israel was living in that region, Reuben went in and slept with his Father's _____ Bilhah, and Israel heard it" (NIV).

SIMEON AND LEVI

Genesis 34:25 states, "Three days later, while all of them were still in pain, two of Jacob's sons, Simeon and Levi, Dinah's brothers, took their swords and _____ the unsuspecting city, killing every male" (NIV).

JUDAH

Proof that Judah possesses an important quality that his older three brothers lacked is found in Genesis 38:26. "Judah recognized them and said, 'She is more _____ than I...'" (NIV).

We also see this quality in Judah in Genesis 44:33, which says, "Now then, please let your servant _____ here as my lord's slave in place of the boy, and let the boy return with his brothers" (NIV).

Judah possesses _____ .

Referring to 1 Peter 5:6, Proverbs 3:34, and James 4:6, humility becomes the quality that enacts and engages God's _____ .

Luke 3:5 says, "Every valley shall be _____ in, every mountain and hill made _____.…" (NIV).

One of the definitions for the word humility (*tapeinoo* in the Greek) is "bringing to the ground, of making level, reducing to a plain. "

1 Peter 5:6 says, "So be content with who you are, and don't put on airs. God's strong hand is on you; He'll _____ you at the right time" (MSG).

What needs to be made low?

What needs to be made high?

What does this mean for me?

_____

_____

_____

_____

Week Three

OXYMORON: RAHAB

[ok-si-mawr-on, -mohr-]

noun, plural oxymora

1.
a figure of speech by which a locution produces
an incongruous, seemingly self-contradictory
effect, as in "cruel kindness" or "to make haste
slowly."

Day One

COINCIDENCE OR DIVINE PROVIDENCE?

And they went and came into the house of a prostitute whose name was Rahab and lodged there" (Joshua 2:1b NIV).

Last week we read about Judah and Tamar, a story containing a scandal that would rival any daytime soap or primetime reality show. It was juicy, and while I enjoy some gossip, I equally revel in the suspense genre. Being a mother of three boys, I have learned to appreciate the intricacies, or in some cases, lack thereof, of a good old-fashioned superhero story. There isn't anything better than watching the good guy defeat the bad guy. It's the classic and irresistible battle of good vs. evil. It sucks us in every time, even though we know how it will most likely end. Perhaps that's why, over the years, there have been over 5,000 superheroes created by Marvel alone. Nothing ignites a little boy's imagination more than a cape and special powers. Boys aside, I admit that I have a favorite superhero also. That may be why I like the story in Joshua's second chapter so much. It's got suspense, danger, an enemy, and an unlikely heroine named Rahab. Let's get to it. Read Joshua 2. As you do, pay attention to the creative way in which the story itself is put together.

Did you notice anything interesting about the composition of this story?

_____

_____

Anyone who thinks that the Bible is boring is crazy. The number of epic stories is unrivaled, and then there's the brilliance of their construction. Every word is important, each story builds to a climax, hinting at the greater story unfolding page by page.

Penned by humans, but clearly inspired by the incomparable creator Himself. You have to love it, or at the very least, respect it. The story in Joshua fits right into that mold. Did you notice how the first paragraph should chronologically come after the second, but its placement at the beginning builds just the right amount of suspense? Do I sound like a theological nerd? Yes? No? Well, if not yet, here's another little tidbit that will throw me into the nerd category indefinitely. Take a moment and note where the two spies come from in verse 1 and write it below.

_____

_____

Now look up a little about this city. Read Numbers 25:1–3 and record your findings in the space provided.

_____

_____

_____

You might have observed that Shittim doesn't exactly have a great reputation in the Israelite community. The people living there bowed down before gods other than their own in clear disobedience to the very first rule recorded in the Ten Commandments, "You shall have no other gods before me" (Exodus 20:3 NIV). I wonder why the author chooses to include this information about Shittim. If I were those two spies, I would have asked specifically for my city of origin to be left out of this narrative. Then I remember, as I mentioned above, that every word in the Scriptures is important and nothing is pure happenstance. I'm led to ask why the city of the two spies, where this despicable event occurred years before, was purposefully included? These spies are about to have an encounter with an ex-harlot. She will ultimately reveal that God is about to fulfill his promise to Moses. They are going to learn that the land guaranteed to them years and years ago is now within their grasp. I wonder if dropping the name of this city isn't just a little bit of foreshadowing. You know that literary device we all learned about in grade school, which appears at the beginning of the story or chapter (true in this case) and helps the reader develop certain expectations about coming events. Perhaps, the reference to Shittim is meant to point us to the story of redemption that God is about to tell here in this chapter and in the Bible as a whole. Don't forget that our heroine is one of the women found in the genealogy of Jesus. It's the ultimate in redemptive placement, if you ask me. Do you think this is as fantastic as I do? Now that all of my cards are on the table, you'll likely agree that I am a theology nerd through and through.

Before we close today, I want to move to another important detail, which might be easily missed, but holds great significance. Reread verse 2 and fill in the following, "And they _____ and _____ into the house of a prostitute, whose name was Rahab and lodged there" (Joshua 2:1 ESV).

Does this statement cause you to ask yourself any important questions? It does me. How did the spies know where to go? Did they have a previous interaction or relationship with her? Did they just stumble upon her place and get exceptionally lucky?

The text helps us to answer a few of these questions. There is no indication of any pre-existing relationship; however, verse 12 clearly communicates that Rahab chose to interact with the spies. Fill in the following from Joshua 2:12, "Now then, please swear to me by the Lord that, as I have dealt _____ with you, so also you will deal kindly with my Father's house…" (ESV).

Is it a coincidence or divine providence that the spies would end up in the home of someone who would deal kindly with them? They could just have easily landed on the doorstep of someone who had a deep sense of patriotism, or even worse, an acute dislike for the Israelites.

Read verse 15 and fill in the following. "Then she let them down by a rope, through the window, for her house was _____ into the _____ wall…" (Joshua 2:15 ESV).

Again, I ask myself, is this a coincidence or divine providence that the woman who took the spies in happened to live in such a strategically beneficial location?

Of course, we can't know for sure that God was behind the scenes orchestrating all of this, but I would put money on it. Have you ever had a situation, which seemed like happenstance, but in hindsight, you could clearly see that God was at work? If so, record it below.

_____

_____

_____

_____

_____

I went out of state for college. Leaving my comfortable, Christian school bubble behind, I learned very quickly that the rest of the world lived a tad bit differently than I was used to. My naïve eyes were opened wide in that first semester of my freshman year. And it wasn't even a state school—it was a Catholic school. Even so, God had my back, as He always does, and introduced me to a girl that would become one of my best friends. I was blessed immensely by her through the next four years. I say, "He introduced" us because, looking back, there was no way that God did not intend for us to meet. Our school mailboxes were right next to each other. She spent the entirety of our college years getting my mail for me due to my total inability to open a coded mailbox. To this day I am totally incompetent when it comes to coded mailboxes; every once and a while I even struggle with regular keys. We both tried out for the rowing team. We lived on the same floor of the same dorm on a campus jam-packed with freshman housing. We chose to attend the same orientation meetings for several extracurricular activities offered on campus. A setup? Is there even a question? For me, there is not. I vividly remember a day that I was distraught and homesick, on the verge of tears; my boyfriend (now husband) was visiting from Point Loma and tried to find the words to comfort me. There she was, popping out of nowhere, and she gave me the biggest bear hug I had ever received. She gives great hugs, and that hug—well it changed things. That hug shifted the current ever so slightly. After that, somewhere deep inside, I knew things were going to be okay.

It's tempting sometimes when things go our way, when everything falls into place, when that stranger says something you really need to hear, or that sermon seems to be written directly for you to write these things off to dumb luck. "That's just a coincidence," we say. But deep down, we feel it. Just like I felt the current change right after my friend's hug, we know that's its Him. The One, the only One, who is as present with us as He was with Adam and Eve in the garden. We experience the care of the One, who guides us and leads us to our promised land. The God who placed those spies in the home of Rahab, places us today. He is just as near to us in the small things, if not more so, than in the big ones. That, dear friends, will lead us into tomorrow's lesson. Coincidence? I doubt it.

God, make us ever aware of Your presence as You lead and guide us. May we see Your hand in all things, great and small. And may we avoid the temptation to write it off as coincidence and praise You instead for Your grace-filled divine providence.

Day Two

HOW STALKS AND FLAX CHANGED EVERYTHING

So here's what I want you to do, God helping you: Take your everyday, ordinary life—your sleeping, eating, going-to-work, and walking-around life—and place it before God as an offering (Romans 12:1 MSG).

In yesterday's lesson, we spent some time discussing the Bible as a whole and how its meticulous attention to detail points to the brilliance of the Creator. God is indeed in the small things, the things that often go unnoticed. And He is very interested in the people who often go overlooked. Today's lesson is proof of that. Go back and read Joshua 2:4–7 to give our lesson some context.

What did Rahab use to hide the spies?

_____

_____

The answer to this question, although seemingly an unimportant detail, actually helps us glean some pertinent information about our female lead character. We learn from verse 2 that Rahab was previously known for her profession. Please write it below in the space provided.

_____

"Rahab, the harlot" was how I knew her prior to my preparation for this Bible study. It's difficult to encounter this name without the label mentioned. According to most scholars, she was a practicing harlot, but she may not have been. According to Matthew

Henry, Rahab, although certainly a prostitute at one point in her past, was no longer one. His commentary states, "Rahab, here called a harlot, a woman that had formerly been of ill fame, the reproach of which stuck to her name, though of late she had repented and reformed."

Whatever her occupation, she had a heart that was prepared.

Back to my previous point. Why is the fact that she hid the spies with stalks of flax an important detail? We know that at this time in history, both wool and flax were critical raw materials used to create clothing. Flax was woven together to make linen and wool woven to make outer garments. In that time, if an Israelite was clothed in linen, he or she was allowed enter into the presence of God. Whether Rahab understood all that or not, God was preparing her to be one of His own.

I can only imagine that if her hope was to no longer be known as "Rahab, the harlot," but simply as "Rahab," it would be a difficult road for her to walk. How hard it must have been for her to remake herself. If even today, she is known not only by her name, but by the label too, how much of a challenge was it to rid herself of this previous identity then? I wonder if, as she heard that knock and met those two spies at her door, she saw it as her way out—her onetime shot. Did she know that welcoming them in might be just the opportunity she needed to create for herself a new name? In hindsight, we know that her actions did accomplish just that. On this side of history, she is known not only by her past, but also by the choice she made in the moment the spies showed up. She is known by her decision to side with the Israelite God.

Can you think of any labels previously or currently attached to you that you wish you could shake? At times these labels may have be positive connotations, but they may now feel negative and wield a feeling of oppression on your life.

_____

_____

I assume we can all come up with a few labels. After every stupid or silly thing I say, there is usually someone asking, "Now, is that a Canadian thing?" This has become my own personal version of the blonde joke. Don't get me wrong! I am proud of my national heritage. It's just that everyone seems to have their own opinions about what it means to be Canadian, and if you don't fit into their predetermined mold, they are confused and bewildered. The conversation can go something like this:

"You don't like mayonnaise?"

"Well, no, I don't. Actually I hate it."

"I thought everyone from Canada ate mayonnaise on everything."

(Insert confused face here.)

Or, "That was rude, I thought everyone from Canada was polite. Are you sure you're from there?"

I kid you not.

I realize that these may be silly examples, but we can all identify with being judged according to a label. I wonder if this is how Rahab felt? Leaving the past behind and moving towards an undetermined and seemingly scary future is not an easy path to take. I wonder if there were moments when Rahab felt unsure, even wrestled with whether or not she was doing the right thing. I picture her walking into the city on a good day, the kind of day where she felt certain she was exactly where she was supposed to be, doing exactly what she was supposed to do. Suddenly she turns a corner, and her eyes recognize a man who is all too familiar. Just when she thought she might have dodged it for the last and final time, her past is thrown back in her face. Do tears roll down her cheeks? Does she wonder, "How will I ever escape it?"

We can identify with that, can't we? It's tough to walk in the present without letting your past mistakes and shame define you. Many of us have asked that same question, "How? How can I possibly move forward when my past haunts me?"

I think the three words, "stalks of flax" help us answer this question. Take a moment and read Proverbs 31:10–31.

What kind of woman is being described here in Proverbs 31:10?

_____

The woman highlighted in that passage is called a wife of noble character. For those of you who are single, don't tune me out here. Many of these principles still apply. You may not have a husband or children that you serve, but I am sure that you have a job, friends, and/or family that you invest your time and energy in. What does verse 13 say the woman does?

_____

_____

"Stalks of flax" shows up here too. This gives us insight into how Rahab was able to push through and answer the "how" question we posed earlier? In light of these verses in Proverbs, what can we learn about Rahab?

_____

_____

How is it that she can move forward from her past and step into her new life? It certainly doesn't happen overnight. It requires waking up every day and taking small steps towards your destination. It requires being diligent in the menial and seemingly unimportant tasks. It requires a refusal to get discouraged with the slow and unnoticed progress. It requires laying down old habits and unhealthy patterns. It requires allowing space and time to breed fertile ground and give birth to new and life giving ones. It's choosing to collect wool and flax instead of opting for the lesser, but often tempting, alternatives.

Do I understand this! Not necessarily because I have a past I am trying to escape, but more so, because cleaning toilets, putting in the laundry, cleaning up the playroom for the millionth time, doing the grocery shopping, washing dishes, carting kids to school and practices, and everything else we stay-at-home moms do has a way of feeling inconsequential from time to time. Or a lot of the time, if I'm being honest. My four closest friends from college have gone on to accomplish some fairly lofty and admirable things: doctor, nurse, lawyer, political lobbyist, and then there's me–captain of the snotty nose and wiper of poopy bottoms extraordinaire. They can brag about saving lives and altering the country's political landscape; I can brag about getting four kids up, dressed, and to church on time or keeping our weekly grocery bill to under one hundred and fifty dollars. Don't get me wrong. These are great accomplishments, but in comparison, they seem to lose their luster. This can ultimately leave me feeling a bit defeated and discouraged from time to time.

Perhaps this is why I get great comfort from this portion of Rahab's story. There she was going about her daily business, participating in the somewhat boring task of collecting wool and flax and laying these fibers out on her roof to dry. Then, in an unexpected turn of events, two spies show up on her doorstep, and before she knows it, she's on her roof hiding them under those very same pieces of wool and flax. In a moment, the meaningless and insubstantial task became profoundly important. What would have happened that day if she hadn't gone out and collected that wool and flax? Where would she have hid them? How would the story have been different? It would have been drastically and radically altered. You see, what gives those routine tasks meaning is their cumulative value—what they added up to over time. My kids won't remember that one time their uniforms were clean for Saturday games or that the kitchen table was wiped and clean before they sat down to the next meal, but they will remember that their mom cared. She cared enough to make sure their sheets were clean. She cared enough to cook them healthy and nutritious meals (even if I did force them to eat that last piece of broccoli). She cared enough to be there not just for the big moments but for the small and insignificant ones, too. For Rahab the payoff was huge. She hid the spies, risking her own life. She spared her family from certain death. Her name is written and will forever exist in the lineage of the one and only true Savior. We don't always see the payoff. Especially not right away. In some cases, we may never see the payoff. But God does. God takes notice. And in Him, it always adds up to something.

Even now, while I try to write, my son is telling me how his gumball, which started out pink, has now turned purple. "Look!" he is saying as he pulls the chewed and saliva-covered gum from his mouth, "It's purple." Sometimes I feel like that piece of gum. Used, abused, and covered in someone else's saliva. The truth is that, day by day, I am being changed from the inside out. Those small tasks I have before me stretch out into what feels like infinity, but they will be the catalyst for change. Pushing me forward, giving space and time for God's work in my life. I don't see the outcome or the solution to the equation, but God does. And today, I trust in that.

Have you ever felt like what you do is inconsequential?

_____

_____

_____

Have you ever felt invisible?

_____

_____

Do you believe that God can use those small and menial tasks for His purposes?

_____

_____

How could this belief give you hope in your present circumstances?

_____

_____

_____

How might God want to change your perspective today?

_____

_____

_____

_____

Let's close with this thought from Romans: "So here's what I want you to do, God helping you: Take your everyday, ordinary life—your sleeping, eating, going-to-work, and walking-around life—and place it before God as an offering" (Romans 12:1 MSG).

Jesus, thank You for being ever present in the big and small of my life. Thank You for seeing everything. Noticing everything. And for changing me, forming me, and molding me, to be more like You through the routine tasks of life. Make me more like You with each unfolding day. I give You my ordinary and place it before You as an offering. Take it and use it for Your good and glory.

Day Three

WHEN THE KING'S ON YOUR DOORSTEP

Unlike the culture around you, always dragging you down to its level of immaturity, God brings the best out of you, develops well-formed maturity in you (Romans 12:2 MSG).

Rahab's faithfulness in the inconsequential and menial tasks opened the door to something greater and more profound in her life. If she had not collected the wool and flax, there may well have been nowhere to hide the spies. If the spies had been captured and not been able to report back to Joshua, the whole mission to take Jericho would have hung in the balance, and the land promised to the Israelites may never have been claimed. The truth is, and it is true for us today, if we are faithful in the small and insignificant things, our diligence can often make way for greatness in our lives and the lives of others.

As we begin today's study, we turn our focus once again to our heroine. She has much to teach us about how to live with our hearts turned towards God, our attention on Him unwavering and unaffected by the culture that surrounds us.

In Joshua 2:2, we learn that the king of Jericho has heard that two Israelite spies have entered the city gates, and that they have made their way to the home of Rahab. Reread verse 3 and answer the following questions.

What does the king ask Rahab to do?

_____

_____

What does she tell the king in verses 4 and 5?

_____

_____

Take a moment and put yourself in Rahab's shoes. Reflect on what she might have been thinking as the king, the *king* of the whole city, shows up on *her* doorstep. She knows that the spies are inside her home and now the king, himself, is asking—no, demanding an account. I am going to ask you to do something that might be a bit out of your comfort zone. Let's participate in a little creative writing exercise. Write what you believe might have been Rahab's inner monologue, as the events we just read unfolded.

Here are some questions to help prompt you in this exercise:

- What might Rahab have been feeling?

    _____

- What influenced Rahab to make the choice she did, in spite of her fears?

    _____

    _____

- In those few seconds, she had to arrive at her decision. Did she question herself? Was she resolute?

    _____

    _____

When the king looks her in the eye and demands to know what she has done with the spies, she chooses to protect them with a lie, all along knowing they are laying under the flax mere feet above their heads. This moment is, without question, the pinnacle of suspense. It's that scene in the movie that you watch with clenched fists on the edge of your seat as the Nazis are searching for the hidden Jews. At every turn they inch closer and closer to discovery spelling the end for the sweet little family hovering behind the bookshelf facade.

I have to hand it to Rahab. She pulls it off. In a moment fraught with danger, one in which I would have fallen apart, she keeps it together. Her choice to keep the spies alive in the face of fear suggests something critical about her character and something even more significant about where her allegiance lies. Her duty to tell the truth to the king of Jericho is outweighed by her desire to honor a different, and in her mind, a much more important King. In yesterday's lesson we closed with reading the beginning of Romans 1. Let's continue reading there today.

> So here's what I want you to do, God helping you: Take your everyday, ordinary life—your sleeping, eating, going-to-work, and walking-around life—and place it before God as an offering. Embracing what God does for you is the best thing you can do for him. Don't become so well-adjusted to your culture that you fit into it without even thinking. Instead, fix your attention on God. You'll be changed from the inside out. Readily recognize what he wants from you, and quickly respond to it. Unlike the culture around you, always dragging you down to its level of immaturity, God brings the best out of you, develops well-formed maturity in you (Romans 1:1–2 MSG).

How does Rahab embody this verse penned by Paul thousands of years after her existence?

_____

_____

Can you identify ways in which you might be so well adjusted to your culture that you fit into it without even thinking?"

_____

_____

_____

Rahab understood that in order for her to embrace something greater she had to let go of the lesser. If she wanted to serve the one true King, she just might have to tell a direct lie in the face of an earthly king who was standing on her doorstep. Her choice should give insight and wisdom into our decision-making process. At times, we, too, have to let go of those things that the world proclaims important to make way for God's work and His priorities in our lives. Our culture will always vie for our attention and allegiance. It lurks at our doorstep, never far from us always ready to pounce if we ever so much as open the door. There will always be a knock, a seemingly honorable suitor there to woo and entice us, but make no mistake, underneath that captivating exterior, are a whole bunch of empty promises. Will we have the same courage that Rahab did and remain faithful to our Betrothed, the only One who can make good on His promise of life—life to the full?

As we continue, read verses 8 through 10. They will provide insight into why Rahab might have hid the spies. In light of these verses, what do you think was her motivation?

_____

_____

Fill in the following blank from the reading: "…I know that the Lord has given you the land, and that the _____ of you has fallen upon us…" (Joshua 2:9 ESV).

Read Psalm 111:1–10. What does verse 10 say is the beginning of wisdom?

_____

_____

Fear. A four-letter word that evokes all sorts of feelings within us, especially when it's placed in the same sentence as God. For many of us, fear has negative connotations. It's what holds us back, it shakes our confidence, and it hinders us from moving forward. It's the emotion that wields the power to glue our feet in place and prohibits us from taking the next step. No question, it *can* be a force of downright destruction in our lives. But this fear, the one talked about by the psalmist, is the kind that leads us to reflect on God and marvel at the great works He has performed in our lives and in the lives of others. It is the fear of the Lord that led the inhabitants of Jericho to say, "We have heard how the Lord dried up the water of the Red Sea before you came out of Egypt, and what you did to the two kings of the amortizes who were beyond the Jordan, to Sihon and Og, whom you devoted to destruction" (Joshua 2:10 ESV). This kind of fear is about acknowledging that God is God and we are not. We come to the end of ourselves and surrender to the possibility that there is something, or, in this case, Someone much greater than us at work. This fear is the beginning of wisdom, the psalmist tells us. Wisdom that reveals to us that we are merely creation in the hands of the almighty Creator. This fear, this openness to something new, this willingness to embrace something greater, led Rahab to make a very bold declaration in the next verse. This will be our focus for tomorrow. For now, let's close in prayer. You can choose to pray the following prayer or simply take some time to respond to what the Spirit of God has done in you today through the study of His Word.

> *Jesus, make me ever aware of where my true allegiance lies. May I not allow my culture to drag me down to immaturity, but instead allow You space to produce well-formed maturity in me. May my heart and attention belong first and foremost to the one and true King and no one else. And may my healthy fear of You lead me to acknowledge that I don't have it all together. Today I proclaim that You are God and I am not. Lead me. I bow to You, and You alone.*

Day Four

THAT GOD, MY GOD

In the same way, faith by itself, if it is not accompanied by action, is dead (James 2:17 NIV).

Yesterday I mentioned the pivotal declarative statement that Rahab made. I want to jump right into with that today. Reread Joshua 2:10 and then fill in the following blanks found in verse 11: "And as soon as we heard it, our hearts _____ and there was no spirit left in any man because of you, for the Lord your God, he _____, in the heavens above and on the earth beneath" (Joshua 2:11 ESV).

In our previous lesson, we talked about how the fear of the Lord is the beginning of wisdom. The fruit produced by this fear is a healthy dose of humility, ultimately causing us to acknowledge and become acquainted with our own limitations. It leads us to open ourselves to the possibility that something or specifically Someone just might be the missing piece to our puzzle. I believe, in my heart, that this is the journey Rahab is taking. For a long time she was convinced that the only means to survival in this difficult and abrasive world was selling herself. There was no other way to make ends meet, but eventually, she arrived at the end of herself. There must have been some sort of defining moment, one that forced her to her knees and caused her to lift her voice to the heavens, crying and begging for a way out, a new life, and a fresh start. Her journey had led her to a fork in the road. She could continue down the same path or be opened to the possibility of a different route. We know which road she chose because of what she says next, "...for the Lord your God, he is God in the heavens above and on the earth beneath" (Joshua 2:11 ESV). Allow me to expound on the text here a bit. Perhaps she thought that God, who led His people out of the land of Egypt through a parted Red Sea and who made a way when there was no way, could make a way for her, too. It was no longer about a third party. This wasn't about a God distant from her current reality. It was about *that* God becoming *her* God.

Can you identify with Rahab? Have you ever come to a place where you knew you didn't have it within yourself to carry on without crying out for help? If so, record it below.

_____

_____

Did that moment lead you to make a similar statement to the one Rahab made? Why or why not?

_____

_____

This statement that Rahab makes, in and of itself, is momentous. She has arrived at a critical juncture and has chosen the path that leads towards God. This is something to celebrate. It's why some followers of Jesus identify a specific moment in time, a decision point when *that* God became *their* God. They may call it their Jesus birthday. It marks a day, not of birth like a normal birthday, but of rebirth. Leaving behind an older way of life, and entering into a new way—becoming a new creation. It's why we get really excited about baptism in our church. Our staff always says when a person is baptized and comes up out of the water, the first thing they should hear is an eruption of clapping. Not golf claps, our pastor often reminds us, but the kind of noise that would bring the house down. Because it's a big deal.

Declarative statements, like the one Rahab made, are great. In fact, they're more than great, they're fantastic. Of course, words quickly lose their potency if actions don't substantiate them. It can often beg the question, was there ever an actual authentic inward change or was it simply a facade of transformation? This doesn't mean that we change overnight or that our former selves, marked by selfishness, turn selfless overnight. It certainly doesn't mean that our past, once defined by vain conceit, vanishes upon command. It's a process. It's why Paul writes, "continue to work out your salvation" (Philippians 2:12 NIV). When a plane takes off and reaches its appropriate elevation, the pilot begins to point it in the direction of its final destination. The pilot knows the desired end, and that is where he heads. Moving in any other direction would seem absurd. When we declare Jesus as the central focus of our lives, we turn from darkness to light. We don't meander; we run towards that light. Who wants to stay in the dark when light is the alternate option? We see in the text that Rahab had truly turned herself towards God, not just in words, but also in deeds. We know that she had a genuine and honest moment of conversion because her statement, "For the Lord your God, he is God" (Joshua 2:11 ESV) is followed directly by her decision to hide the spies. Her works showed the evidence.

Take a moment and read James 2:14–26. Fill in the following blank: "In the same way, faith by itself, if not accompanied by _____ is _____" (James 2:17 NIV).

The Message puts it this way, "Isn't it obvious that God talk without God acts is outrageous?" (James 2:17 MSG). On my way to drop my older boys off at VBS last summer, I promised my younger son that if he came with me to drop off his brothers at their classrooms, without complaining or throwing fits, we could go to the play area at the mall. I have to admit I use bribery a lot with my kids, and this day was no exception. I had just given birth to my daughter a month earlier and was breastfeeding what felt like every three minutes. As many of you may know, nothing gives you cabin fever more than having a newborn. I needed an outing just as much as my son did, if not more. So, when he stubbornly refused to get out of the car and made me drag him, kicking and screaming, while I struggled to push Abby in her stroller all the way to the classrooms, I was faced with a decision. I could either forget what I said about not throwing a fit being the determining factor for whether we did or did not go to the play area or, begrudgingly, I could let my yes be yes and my no be no and head back to our house as I had said I would do under the circumstances. It was tough, harder than it probably should have been, but I turned left out of the parking lot towards home instead of turning right towards the mall.

That's the trick isn't it? Words are great. Promises are a wonderful thing to make. But if they are not followed by action, they hold no meaning. They are void of substance and significance and therefore, worthless. If we make it a pattern of not following through, at some point, no one will believe a word we say. James is pretty serious about this idea that words should be backed up by actions because the stakes are extra high when it comes to our beliefs. Nothing is a greater turn off to those outside the faith than Christians who are hypocritical and full of empty promises.

Can you think of a time when your words were not backed up by your actions?

_____

_____

Can you think of a time when your words were backed by your actions?

_____

_____

What were the positive and negative consequences of each of these scenarios?

_____

In what area of your life, today, is God calling you to follow through on your word? What steps can you take to ensure change?

_____

_____

Day Five

A RED CORD

In the same way, let your light shine before men, that they may see your good deeds, and praise your Father in heaven (Matthew 5:16 NIV).

We ended yesterday by discussing the importance of letting our inward declarations give way to outward change in our lives. Today, we will finish our story of Rahab and the spies. Let's pick up in verse 12 and read until the end of Joshua 2.

According to verse 18, what color cord was it that the spies requested Rahab to tie in the window of her home?

_____

For a Jewish audience, that color and the placement of the cord itself would immediately remind them of another story in the Old Testament. Can you think of what story I am referring?

_____

If you wrote Passover, then you are brilliant and correct. If you are not familiar with this story, or even if you are, turn to Exodus 12 and read through the first thirteen verses. Answer the following questions as we attempt to draw some connections from the time of Moses to the time of Rahab, and right on to the time of Jesus. What was it the Israelites were to put on their doorframes in order for the plague of the firstborn to pass over them?

_____

Take it a step further and read Matthew 26:2. What was Jesus preparing to do at the time of Passover?

_____

_____

Read Matthew 26:17. What meal, a ritual that we practice today in the church, was Jesus about to participate in on the day of Passover?

_____

_____

Stay with me. We are building to something, and it requires some work at the forefront. Continue by reading the following, which is an excerpt from Hebrews 9.

> But when the Messiah arrived, high priest of the superior things of this new covenant, he bypassed the old tent and its trappings in this created world and went straight into heaven's "tent"—the true Holy Place—once and for all. He also bypassed the sacrifices consisting of goat and calf blood, instead using his own blood as the price to set us free once and for all. If that animal blood and the other rituals of purification were effective in cleaning up certain matters of our religion and behavior, think how much more the blood of Christ cleans up our whole lives, inside and out. Through the Spirit, Christ offered himself as an unblemished sacrifice, freeing us from all those dead-end efforts to make ourselves respectable, so that we can live all out for God (Hebrews 9:11–15 MSG).

How did Jesus become the Passover Lamb?

_____

_____

I don't think it's a coincidence that the cord Rahab tied on her window was red. It would have, undoubtedly, caused the Jews to reflect and recall God's faithfulness that Passover day in Egypt when all of the Israelite's firstborn children were spared. They would have easily connected the dots from Egypt to Jericho, and worshipped the God who not only spared Rahab and her family, but fulfilled another promise. The promise I am referring to is granting them access to the land that was rightfully theirs. We read these stories, on this side of the cross, and for us, they point to an even greater reality. We can connect the final dot—the most significant moment in the history of humanity. The God of Moses and Rahab is a God who spares His people. That God is our God. He stops at nothing to ensure that His people inherit the kind of life He has always intended for them. He has bestowed upon us the blessing promised to Abraham and his descendants (us) in Genesis 12. This same blessing is written about by Paul in his letter to the Ephesians, "How blessed is God! And what a blessing he is!…Long before he laid down the earth's foundations, he has us in mind, settled on us as the focus of his love" (Ephesians 1:3–4 MSG). He has done all this, in spite of what it cost Him—the sacrifice of His one and only Son. Jesus becomes the Passover Lamb, and through his blood, we are spared from the destruction our sin inevitably causes in our lives and from the death we rightfully deserve.

The blood smeared over the Israelites' doorways in Egypt and the scarlet cord hung in Rahab's window is what set them apart. This caused the Israelites to stand out and became the defining quality separating them from the rest. This distinction would be what ultimately saved their lives. Jesus does this for us. His blood covers us, sets us apart, and saves us. Praise God! However, there's a catch. Of course, this catch, unlike most, is beautiful, stunning, and gives our lives deep meaning and purpose. He doesn't set us apart and save us merely for us, and us alone. He does it so that our lives might, in turn, be marked by some sort of defining quality as well. That we, too, might begin to possess characteristics separating us from the world. That we, who are blessed, might become a blessing. Our lives were always meant to be a picture or glimpse of the God who gave us that abundant life in the first place. Let's see this scenario played out in the Scriptures. Read the following passages and briefly write how they tie into our discussion.

Ephesians 2:8–10

_____

_____

1 Peter 2:11–12

_____

_____

Matthew 5:16

_____

_____

1 John 4:12

_____

_____

When we allow ourselves to be marked by Jesus and His ways, the invisible is made visible. When we walk in the light and the love He gives us, others cannot help but take note.

I was on the rowing team for my first two years of college. Every weekday morning my alarm went off at 4:45 a.m., and I stumbled out of bed, threw on clothes, hopped into my car, and made my way to the boathouse in the pitch black. My teammates and I, still half asleep, would lift our boat up and over our heads and take it to the edge of the water. We then endured what I thought was the very worst part of practice—the icy chill of water crawling up over our toes and making its way over our ankles—as we gently laid the boat in the water. It gives me shivers now just thinking about it. As we began our workout and the sun would begin to creep up over the horizon, the chill quickly subsided. The water might have been extremely cold on our toes, but the payoff, a front row seat as the sun made its daily debut, was always worth it. Because that is what light does. It creeps in. Before you know it, it has taken over. It gives new life to everything and brings hope to the dark places. There's no escape from it, and there is no way to dispute the change it brings. And it does change things. Objects are not the same in light as they are in darkness. They are marked by something different, and the evidence the light leaves in its wake is difficult to ignore.

The word *melt* is used three separate times Rahab's story. Glance back quickly to the text of Joshua 2 and take note of the three usages. It is interesting, considering that is one of the effects that light has on its surroundings. When the temperature is right, there is not much snow can do to combat the sun's rays beating down upon it. Similarly, there really wasn't much the inhabitants of Jericho could do to dispute or ignore the great works of God. "As soon as we heard it," the Scripture says, "our hearts melted" (Joshua 2:11 ESV). For Rahab, this light penetrated her heart; her words became evidence of this work of light when she declared, "…your God, he is God in the heavens above and on the earth beneath" (Joshua 2:11 ESV). That same light, which burned bright within her, changes not only her destiny, but the fate of the spies and consequently the fate of the entire nation of Israel. In Joshua 2:24, what do the spies report to Joshua, son of Nun?

_____

_____

_____

Light cannot be contained. It made its way into the heart of Rahab, the harlot, changing her from the inside out and forever altering the world around her. I wonder if Joshua would have felt confident to proceed in his God-given quest to take hold of the Promised Land, had it not been for God's work in Rahab and her obedient response to that work. We can see now why her name belongs in the genealogy. She leaves quite a legacy. Rahab later becomes the mother of Boaz, who is the father of Obed, the father of King David. King David is the king who would make way for the one and only true King. You see, light, in its very nature, cannot be contained. It seeps from generation to generation to generation. And its effects are lasting and profound.

What would it look like to invite that light into your soul? What kind of changes would it lead you towards?

_____

_____

_____

How could that same light become a beacon of hope for future generations?

_____

_____

_____

How can you run into the Light, in the particular circumstances that surround you today?

_____

_____

_____

> *Jesus, You are the One and True Light of the world. The only One who can really bring hope to the dark places of our lives. Shine Your light in my life. Change me from the inside out. And let that light effect change not just in me but through me. May my life point others towards You and bring You the glory You so well deserve.*

Video Session Four
THE HARLOT HEROINE

INTRODUCTION

Oxymoron is defined as a location that produces an incongruous. Which really means a word or a phrase that is _____, or not harmonious in

_____.

Brennan Manning makes the following statement:

> When I get honest, I admit I am a _____ of
> _____. I believe and I doubt, I hope and get discouraged, I love and I hate, I feel bad about feeling good, I feel guilty about not feeling guilty. I am trusting and suspicious. I am honest and I still play games. Aristotle said I am a rational animal; I say I am an angel with an incredible capacity for beer.
>
> To live by grace means to acknowledge my whole life story, the light side and the dark. In admitting my shadow side I learn who I am and what God's grace means. As Thomas Merton put it, "A saint is not someone who is good but who experiences the goodness of God.

THE HALL OF HEROES (HEBREWS 11)

Hebrews 11:31 says, "By faith the prostitute Rahab, because she _____ the spies, was not killed with those who were disobedient" (NIV).

Rahab teaches us that we must welcome or receive (as the KJV states) _____.

Risk leads to extraordinary change in the life of Rahab in several ways:

1) She becomes a part of the _____.

2) She marries _____ (one of the spies).

3) She becomes an Israelite _____.

4) She becomes the grandmother of _____.

Hebrews 11:1 says, "The fundamental fact of existence is that this trust in God, this faith, is the firm _____ under everything that makes this life _____ living" (MSG).

Risk ➡ Change ➡ Increased Faith

Hebrews 11:31 says, "By faith the harlot Rahab perished not with them that believed when she had received the spies with _____" (KJV).

What does this mean for me?

_____

_____

_____

_____

_____

_____

_____

_____

_____

_____

_____

_____

_____

Week Four

FORESHADOWING: RUTH

[fawr-shad-oh, fohr-]

verb (used with object)

   1.

to show or indicate beforehand; prefigure:

Day One

NAOMI

If your heart is broken, you'll find God right there. If you're kicked in the gut, he'll help you catch your breath (Psalm 34:18 MSG).

Welcome to our fourth week of study together. It's my hope and prayer that you've read the stories of our heroines and through the study of their lives, found God moving in your own. They have certainly taught me a great deal and propelled me to ask some important and poignant personal questions. It's my desire that this week be no different. If you recall, at the end of our study last week, I mentioned that Rahab was the mother of Boaz. It's with his story, and with the story of the woman who unexpectedly showed up in his life, that we begin today. So far, our stories have shocked us with their drama and scandal and forced us to the edge of our seats in suspense. There is no debating that the book of Ruth reads much like a good romance novel, one that might even pique the interest of Nicholas Sparks fans. I mean, is there anyone else who has watched *The Notebook* more times than they can count? I'm a sucker for Ryan Gosling just as much as the next girl. Can I get an "amen"?

Our previous stories have been centered on one chapter of Scripture, but this week's story is comprised of four chapters and earns its very own book in the Old Testament. Today we focus on Ruth 1. (Please note that I have used the ESV version and it will help if you are able to access this version as you read and fill in the blanks.) Ruth 1:1–5 serves as the introduction, reveals the backstory, and communicates to us some of the key characters. Fill in the following character graph to help you get the family tree straight in your head. I found this exercise helpful in my personal study, as I can easily lose track of who's who when it comes to some of the ancient Hebrew names and locations. I hope you find it beneficial as well.

FAMILY TREE

( )   ( )

( )   (Mahlon)   ( )   ( )

Where does Elimelech leave from and arrive to?

_____

_____

The city from which they depart is the setting of another very famous story. Any idea what that story might be?

_____

_____

What happens at the end of verse 5?

_____

_____

Naomi, Ruth, and Orpah are all that remains of this family. Let's find out what the women decide to do. Read the remainder of the chapter, and as you read, take note of any words that are repeated more than once. I have included some of the repeating words you may uncover below. Tally the number of times you find each of these words and answer the questions below.

my daughters: _____ times

wept: _____ times

What do these two words tell us about the relationship between Naomi and her two daughter's-in-law?

_____

_____

bitter: _____ times

How does Naomi feel about her unfortunate circumstances?

_____

_____

Searching for repeated words is another strategy I use when studying Scripture because it frequently points to significant themes. It is the writer's way of drawing the reader's attention to certain portions they believe are of critical importance. It's as if the repeated words and phrases beckon to us. "Focus here!" they cry out, "You won't want to miss this!" You might have noticed that the author refers both Ruth and Orpah as Naomi's daughters-in-law, but when the verses shift to the voice of Naomi, she calls them "my daughters." Not once, not twice, but three separate times. This isn't exactly indicative of a typical relationship between in-laws. I happen to have a great relationship with my husband's mother, but a good number of my friends can't say the same thing. After the death of Naomi's husband and her two sons, can you even fathom it? She feels she has nowhere else to go, but home to her birthplace. She urges both Ruth and Orpah to return to the home of their mothers and make a new life for themselves, too. However, in an interesting turn of events, they both refuse. It becomes apparent that not only does Naomi view them as daughters, but that they, in turn, feel a greater allegiance to their mother-in-law than to their own mothers. The thought of leaving dear Naomi, whom they have come to love and value so highly, moves them to tears two separate times in the text. Eventually, Orpah is convinced and surrenders to the pleas of Naomi, but Ruth remains steadfast and determined to remain at Naomi's side.

This leads us to one of the most beautiful passages in the book of Ruth—Ruth's passionate declaration to her most treasured Naomi. She says, "Don't urge me to leave you or to turn back from you. Where you go I will go, and where you stay I will stay.

Your people will be my people and your God my God. Where you die I will die, and there I will be buried. May the Lord deal with me, be it ever so severely, if even death separates you and me" (Ruth 1:16–17 NIV).

Moving, isn't it? In the ten years the women have spent together, Ruth has observed Naomi. She has watched her serve her family and her community, have her noble and virtuous character tested, and prove herself faithful over and over again. Naomi is unwavering in her devotion to the Lord. She provided stability for Ruth. Something her daughter-in-law had most likely not been exposed to prior to her joining the family. It seems, as a result of her direct mentorship over her adopted daughter, Ruth has found refuge and security in the God of Naomi. Perhaps Ruth discovered through Naomi's life and testimony that this God could provide her with something the Moabite gods simply could not. It's a beautiful relationship these two women share, and I can't help but ponder as I write if the way in which I carry myself and how I live is leaving in its wake the kind of lasting influence that Naomi's did? Let's take a moment and consider this question. Has God used you to turn another's life towards Him?

_____

_____

_____

Naomi is inspiring, isn't she? We are inspired in more ways than one, but the other word that we see more than a few times is bitter. Clearly, the loss of both her husband and her two sons has left her utterly and completely devastated. I, for one, can't even comprehend such a tragedy. Perhaps that is why she cries out in verse 13 and says, "No, my daughters, for it is exceedingly bitter to me for your sake that the hand of the Lord has gone out against me" (ESV). Life has been so difficult for Naomi and taken such a toll on her. So much so, that when she returns to her native land, the women, who were most likely some of her closest friends before her departure, ask what question? Refer to verse 19.

A woman, whom they most likely were intimately acquainted with, is no longer recognizable to them. She even asks them to call her by a new name. Fill in the following blanks. "Do not call me _____ call me _____ for the Almighty has death very _____ with me" (Ruth 1:20 ESV).

Have you ever felt that way before? Has the hand life dealt you ever been so tough or oppressive, that you've looked up and shook your fist to God saying, "How could You have done this to me? Surely Your hand is against me." If you can identify with this sentiment, fill in your experiences in the blanks below:

_____

_____

_____

_____

_____

Life has ravaged, wrecked, and laid waste to Naomi. She feels beyond distraught. But what is most impressive about her character, beyond even how Ruth and Orpah feel about her, is how she responds in the face of her impossibly difficult circumstances. Her words might go out against the Lord, but her actions tell a different story. Go back, read verse 6, and fill in the following: "Then she arose with her daughters-in-law to return from the country of Moab, for she had heard in the fields of Moab that the _____ had _____ his people..." (Ruth 1:6 ESV).

She heard that the Lord was with His people in Bethlehem and she decided to go there. Instead of running from God, she moved in the only direction she knew could save her—towards Him. Easier said than done. When life lays waste to us, it may seem like the best solution, the most logical one, is to lay blame at the feet of the only One who we deem able to stop the tragedy from striking in the first place. So, we cry out against Him and run the other direction. The truth is, He is the only One that can save us. When life has emptied us, He's the only One that can fill us again. As we continue to read, we will come to see that God does just that for Naomi. Let's close with these questions:

Do you believe that turning towards God as opposed to running away from Him is the right choice? If not, explain. If so, explain.

_____

_____

_____

_____

_____

Have you ever experienced Psalm 34:18 to be true for you or witnessed its truth in the life of someone you know? "If your heart is broken, you'll find God right there. If you're kicked in the gut, he'll help you catch your breath" (Psalm 34:18 MSG).

Turn to Him, sisters, don't run. Life can leave us battered and bruised, but only the true Healer can bring restoration and wholeness.

Day Two

THE IMPRESSIVE RÉSUMÉ OF BOAZ

But God put his love on the line for us by offering his Son in sacrificial death while we were of no use whatsoever to him (Romans 5:8 MSG).

Yesterday we looked at Naomi's character, her relationships with her daughters-in-law, and her choice to move towards God instead of away from Him in the midst of her very painful and difficult circumstances. Today, we move to the second chapter of Ruth, which introduces us to another of our story's lead characters. What is his name and what do we learn about him in Ruth 2:1?

_____

_____

_____

What specific adjective is used to describe him?

_____

The dictionary defines the word *worthy* as having adequate or great merit; character or value. I don't think there is any coincidence that worthy is the word used to describe Boaz in the very first moment that we are introduced to him. The remainder of the chapter reads a lot like a résumé—a very impressive, character-revealing résumé. Boaz was worthy, not only of Ruth, but of his place in history, as the great-grandfather of King David. He would be the one to prepare the way for the true and rightful king. The One who would eventually enter the picture and whose rule would alter the relationship between God and humanity forever.

We will spend the remainder of our time today looking at what might be considered bullet points on the résumé of Boaz, one of Ruth and Naomi's redeemers. We will then examine how these characteristics foreshadow our true Redeemer. Read Ruth 2:2–4.

What is Ruth doing in these two verses?

_____

In whose field does she end up? _____

Ruth is gleaning in the fields after the reapers. In other words, she is collecting grain that has been left behind by those in charge of its gathering. Leviticus 19:9–10 provides insight into why we find her participating in this particular activity. Read it, and then, in the blank below, write the résumé's first bullet point with what you have observed about the character of Boaz through these verses.

1) _____

> The first word that comes to my mind is obedience and perhaps you landed on that same word or one like it. Boaz is obedient to God's law. 1 John 5:3 says, "For this is the love of God, that we keep his commandments. And his commandments are not burdensome" (Esv). Basically, we see Boaz's love for God revealed through His obedience. Not only that, but it's through his obedience that Ruth is given a chance to provide for herself and for Naomi.

As we move forward with our lesson for today, we will continue to fill in Boaz's hypothetical résumé and then examine ways the character of Boaz mirrors the character of Jesus. Read Philippians 2:6–8. What same word we have just mentioned above is found in concordance with Jesus. What is the context?

_____

_____

Jesus is obedient to the point of death, even death on a cross. Another way of putting it is there were no limits to the depth and breadth of His obedience. When we meet Boaz in verse 4 of Ruth 2, we learn that he is a relative of Naomi coming from Bethlehem much like Elimelech. Of course, we aren't told this in the text, but it is believed by scholars that Boaz is quite a bit older than Ruth. Perhaps closer in age to her father-in-law. So, it is fairly likely that Boaz endured the same famine in the land that his relative, Elimelech, had. The difference being that Elimelech fled with his family and Boaz remained in Bethlehem. Boaz chose to stay in the land purely because He knew it was God's land. For him, there was wisdom in remaining in a place where the people of God dwelt and God Himself was present. In order to remain pure and set apart as the Law encouraged him, Boaz was unwilling to open himself up to the influence of outsiders even during famine. You may recall that in a previous lesson we discussed the importance of sticking together in order to remain set apart. Boaz was obedient, even if, at times, it threatened his very life.

Continuing on in verses 4 and 5, we get great insight into how Boaz treats his servants. Fill in our second bullet point as you think about how his relationship with his servants, and the interest he takes in the strange woman gleaning in his field, reveals about his upstanding and worthy character.

2) _____

The kind of greeting that Boaz gives to his reapers is telling. These are men that work for him. As many of us know from personal experience, those who are above us in the overall hierarchy of life can often choose to mistreat those under them. This can occur in both public and private life. It can occur with a superior at work or an elder in our family. Those placed in positions of authority must take caution to avoid the abuse of power. However, Boaz does not take this path. He opts for a way of respect and dignity instead. James 1:27 says this, "Religion that God our father accepts as pure and fault-less is this: to look after orphans and widows in their distress…" (NIV). By watching out for Ruth, as we will see Boaz continually does throughout the remainder of this chapter, he passes the test of true religion outlined in the book of James.

In Luke 4, we are told that Jesus was teaching in a synagogue in Nazareth, the town in which he grew up. He read from a scroll, quoting Isaiah, but really gave what might be termed as His mission statement or the purpose of His ministry. Read verses 18–19 of Luke 4. Sum it up below.

_____

_____

_____

Now, take a moment to read Ruth 2: 6–18 and record any similarities you might find between the mission statement of Jesus and the actions of Boaz from our story. Take careful note of *all* the ways Boaz cares for Ruth and for Naomi. There are many.

_____

_____

_____

_____

_____

Boaz goes above and beyond, doesn't he? He watches out for Ruth, ensures she is protected, makes sure that she eats and is satisfied, and concerns himself with the needs of Naomi as well. He speaks kind and encouraging words to Ruth and compliments her for her dedication to her mother-in-law. Perhaps at this point there are some romantic feelings beginning to develop between the two. Some scholars may argue in favor of this, but I believe this is how he would have treated any and all of his servants. His worthy character proves itself over and over again.

As we move to the final point on the hypothetical résumé of Boaz, read verse 20 and examine what Naomi calls him at the very end of the verse. Then write this word in the blank below.

3) _____

Ruth is in a difficult situation—a fairly dire predicament, if you ask me. In this extremely patriarchal culture and time, the fact that she is not attached to a man leaves her extraordinarily vulnerable. The only person she has to call family is Naomi, and Naomi is a widow, too. Perhaps this is why Ruth seems quite shocked by the abundant kindness shown to her by Boaz. Fill in the following blanks from the statements made about Boaz.

Ruth 2:10: "Why have I found favor in your eyes, that you should take notice of me, since I am a _____?" (ESV).

Ruth 2:13: "I have found favor in your eyes, my lord, for you have comforted me spoken kindly to your servant, though I am not one of your _____" (ESV).

Ruth 2:19: "Blessed be the man who _____ _____ of you" (ESV).

Boaz takes notice of Ruth, although she is a woman and a foreigner. He treats her with kindness and dignity, and he does for her what she could not do for herself. He gives her a chance at a new, better life. Ultimately, isn't that what Jesus did for us? Those of us who are Gentiles, not Jews by birth or ancestry, were once considered foreigners ourselves. Read Ephesians 2:11–13, 19.

Who has brought us near to God?

_____

In verse 19, what are we called now?

_____

God exerts the greatest amount of kindness towards us by drawing us near to Him through the blood of Jesus Christ.

Christ arrives right on time to make this happen. He didn't, and doesn't, wait for us to get ready. He presented himself for this sacrificial death when we were far too weak and rebellious to do anything to get ourselves ready. And even if we hadn't been so weak, we wouldn't have known what to do anyway. We can understand someone dying for a person worth dying for, and we can understand how someone good and noble could inspire us to selfless sacrifice. But God put his love on the line for us by offering his Son in sacrificial death while we were of no use whatsoever to him (Romans 5:6–8 MSG).

Just as Boaz intercedes for Ruth at her weakest and most vulnerable moment, Christ, at just the right moments, intercedes for us! Don't miss the good news here. While we were running from Christ, turning our backs on Him, and choosing our own way, He paid the ultimate sacrifice. He did for us what we absolutely could not do for ourselves. He gave us the greatest gift: value, dignity, life everlasting and life to the fullest. We can proclaim, just as Naomi did of Boaz, "Blessed be the man, who took notice of me!" (Ruth 2:19 NIV).

Some of you have heard the message of the gospel thousands of times before. If so, let Romans 3 fall afresh on you today. If this story is new to you, let the depth of this wholly wonderful truth transform you. Let's rejoice for we "See what great love the Father has lavished on us, that we should be called children of God!" (1 John 3:1 NIV). Meditate on that. Revel in that. Like a child clings to the feet of its mother, let's press into God today. Let's thank Him for His kindness towards us and for doing for us what we could not do for ourselves. Write your response to this good news and to Romans 3 in the space below:

_____

_____

_____

_____

_____

Day Three

ALL THAT YOU SAY, I WILL DO

*And let us consider how we may spur one another on toward love
and good deeds* (Hebrews 10:24 NIV).

Yesterday, we noticed the kindness Boaz showed in his dealings with Ruth. This
ultimately led us to reflect and consider how much greater and more profound
God's kindness is towards us. As we move to the third chapter of our story, we will
settle in on the first five verses. Please read Ruth 3:1–5 now and fill in the blank. "My
daughter, should I not seek _____ for you that it may be well with you?"
(Ruth 3:1 ESV)

This sentence is of utmost importance because it's a window into the heart of Naomi.
It gives us a look at her inner motivations and sheds light on why she offers the advice
she does to her dear daughter, Ruth. That word *rest* is also used in Ruth 1:9. Go back
and read this verse. What does Naomi's hope her daughters-in-law will find?

_____

_____

She longs for them to find new husbands and for the pain and anguish they experienced because of the deaths of Mahlon and Chilion to have some redemptive value.
In her heart of hearts, she wants what is best for them both. Naomi reasserts this hope
in chapter 3. If Ruth is ever going to be able to let her guard down, to be protected,
loved, and cherished, if she is ever going to be able to find peace, Naomi knows it will
come through a redeemer. In this case, Boaz.

Let's take this time to make a list of the actions Naomi gives Ruth to accomplish the
night she goes to see Boaz.

1) _____

2) _____

3) _____

4) _____

5) _____

6) _____

7) _____

8) _____

Quite the list, isn't it? I want you to know, first and foremost, that there is nothing that Naomi tells Ruth to do that is scandalous or of lewd intent. Her instructions align perfectly with the laws of the Torah. Boaz is in fact Ruth's kinsman redeemer, and it is within her rights and responsibilities to make this known to him. Lying down at the feet of Boaz and uncovering his feet was a well-known practice in that day and time. A servant often performed a similar action towards his or her master, indicating total and full submission to them. Of course, you have to laugh a little at the embellishments Naomi adds. I'm not sure about you, but it tickles my fancy a bit. It's as if she has said, "Go ahead and get dolled up, put on your best perfume, and dress in your most beautiful garment. Then wait it out. Don't get ahead of yourself or overexcited. But hold off making contact with him until he has eaten and had a drink and is in good spirits." Perhaps she whispers to her quietly and under her breath, "We ladies know that a man is much happier, less grumpy, and certainly easier to deal with if they have eaten. Seek out the place he goes to lay down, uncover his feet, and lie down. He'll know immediately that your intentions are honorable and he will tell you what to do next."

That Naomi, she's pretty quick, isn't she? If you ask me, Naomi gives Ruth some extremely wise counsel that I'm guessing Ruth would not have arrived at on her own. Naomi knew the Israelite laws inside and out. She knew what was within their rights and the proper way to go about petitioning for those rights. She had a greater understanding of the big picture and was able to discern Ruth's next steps, advising her accordingly.

It's so important, isn't it? To have people around us that we trust indefinitely, who have proved over and over again that they have our best interests in mind. People we can invite into our inner lives, reveal our secrets to, and who can share in our greatest vulnerabilities. People who have seen us at our worst and at our best. People who can encourage us when we most need it, reprimand us as required, speak the truth if necessary, challenge us when a kick in the behind is needed, and celebrate with us when victories and dreams are achieved. We need accountability. We need community. The bottom line is that human beings were made to exist in deep partnership with one another. It's why God proclaims, after He has completed the creation of the first man, "It is not good for man to be alone. I will make a helper suitable for him" (Genesis 2:18 NIV). And it's why Solomon, the wisest man to ever live, apart from Jesus, said this, "Two are better than one, because they have a good return for their labor: If either of them falls down, one can help the other up. But pity anyone who falls and has no one to help them up. Also, if two lie down together, they will keep warm. But how can one keep warm alone? Though one may be overpowered, two can defend themselves. A cord of three strands is not quickly broken (Ecclesiastes 4:9–12 NIV).

Scripture is pretty clear about the importance of seeking wise counsel and accountability through intimate and trusted relationships. Look up the following verses and write a brief synopsis in the blanks provided.

Proverbs 1:5 _____

_____

Proverbs 11:14 _____

_____

Proverbs 12:15 _____

_____

Proverbs 19:20 _____

_____

1 Corinthians 15:33 _____

_____

Colossians 3:16 _____

_____

In Proverbs, Solomon doesn't mince words. I'm paraphrasing here, but he basically comes right out and says, "Fact: if you ignore the counsel of the wise, you are and will be considered stupid." As I stare into my computer screen, typing these words, my heart is filled with a God-given, Spirit-led conviction. There is one word I can't seem to shake and it is *intentional*. When it comes to these relationships and friendships, we have to be intentional. They aren't formed by accident and don't flourish without attention and time. They don't just fall into our lap without any effort on our part. If we don't make them a priority, we will not only miss out, but the lack of deep interpersonal relationships can be damaging to our soul. Answer the following questions with as much ruthless candor as you can possibly muster. I promise you, I will do the same.

Do you believe in the importance of outside and wise counsel?

_____

_____

Do you now, or have you ever had, a person in your life you feel you can trust and feel comfortable with revealing even your most intimate vulnerabilities? Keep in mind, if you are married it is good to have this kind of honesty with your spouse. However, it is important that you have someone else, usually of the same sex, you feel you can be honest with also.

_____

_____

_____

Are you able to get together with this person with regularity? I recognize our lives are busy with jobs, kids, spouses, other family, etc. If not, what steps can you take to ensure this will happen?

_____

_____

_____

_____

Are you in the habit of seeking wise counsel from others with a greater and broader perspective than yours, when it comes to the larger and weightier decisions in life?

_____

_____

_____

_____

You will remember from our text that after Naomi gives her advice to Ruth, Ruth replies, "All that you say I will do" (Ruth 3:5 ESV). Wise counsel is only helpful if we are willing to listen and apply it to our lives. Are you willing to listen and really hear both encouragement and constructive criticism without disregarding or evading either one?

_____

_____

_____

To close today, if you have read through these questions and feel ill-equipped to answer them because you don't have any relationships that meet the qualifications discussed above, begin now by praying that God would do one of two things:

1) Make you aware of an already existing friendship and help you to take intentional steps towards developing greater levels of accountability.

2) Ask God to bring someone into your life who might be able to fill this void. Be alert and attuned to how He is leading you. Perhaps you need to get further connected in your church, in a small group, or a Bible study.

> I am praying for you, dear friends, and for myself as well. This journey of walking with Jesus is far from easy; in fact, it's incredibly challenging and difficult. We need each other. Let me rephrase: we desperately need each other. To quote the words of Paul in his letter to the Ephesians, "And let us consider how we may spur one another on toward love and good deeds" (Hebrews 10:24 NIV). Let us consider it carefully.

Day Four

IS HE WORTHY?

Our Father in heaven, hallowed be your name, your kingdom come,
your will be done, on earth as it is in Heaven (Matthew 6:9–10 NIV).

In yesterday's lesson, we focused on Ruth 3:1–6. We witnessed Naomi's wise counsel towards Ruth and gained clear insight into her heart and motivation. Naomi, indeed, wished for rest and peace for her daughter, Ruth—a woman whom she loved with such devotion and tenderheartedness. Having Ruth's best interests at heart, Naomi's love was clearly selfless in its intent. Today let's turn to the remainder of the chapter. Read Ruth 3: 7–18 and then fill in the blank from verse 9: "He said, 'Who are you?' And she answered, 'I am Ruth, your _____. Spread your wings over your servant, for you are a _____'" (Ruth 3:9 ESV).

The sentence above will serve as a theme for today's lesson. If you remember from Day 2 of this week, we focused our attention on Boaz and observed some keen similarities between him, Ruth's redeemer, and Jesus, our Redeemer. Today we will carry on using this metaphor. Assuming that Boaz represents Jesus in our story who, then, does Ruth represent?

_____

_____

If Ruth represents us, then Ruth's response in verse 9 gives us discernment into how we should respond to Jesus in our lives. Let's take some time to really unpack verse 9. How does Ruth identify herself to Boaz?

_____

She acknowledges that she is the lesser—the one possessing limited power and authority with fewer rights—and places herself in submission to Boaz. She knows her role and acknowledges it as such. When she speaks, she calls herself his servant, and her actions prove it. We previously learned why Naomi advised Ruth to lay at Boaz's feet. Write what you can recall about why she did and reference back to it, if necessary.

_____

_____

Ruth has gleaned in his fields, listened to his instruction, and then reveals her allegiance completely, by laying at his feet. This, also, is to be our posture towards our Lord Jesus.

When Jesus walked this earth, He gave a famous sermon in which He taught us how to pray. Although I'm sure most of you could recite it by heart, turn to Matthew 6:9–13 and write the first five lines in the space provided.

_____

_____

_____

_____

Now, if you were to rephrase this in today's language, how would it read? Write your interpretation below.

_____

_____

_____

I think for me, it would be seven simple words going something like this: You are God, and I am not. Jesus knew the importance of acknowledging repeatedly that we must begin every prayer with a bowed knee and a submissive heart. Hallowed be *Your* name, *Your* kingdom come, *Your* will be done. I am detecting a theme: *Yours*, Lord, not *mine*.

Now some of you may be thinking, Why? Why would Ruth submit to Boaz in that way? Why would she deliberately choose to put herself in such a vulnerable position, one in which she could so easily be taken advantage of? Maybe some of you have been burned more times than you would like to admit because you chose to place your trust in a person who ultimately betrayed you. I get it. I really do. But I'll tell you why Ruth does what she does. It's why we have the backstory. Boaz is a man of upstanding character. Maybe you remember that little adjective used to describe him in the beginning of Ruth 2, *worthy*. He is a worthy man and worthy of Ruth's trust. She submits to him because he is kind, good, and treats her with the honor, respect, and dignity that she deserves. Turn to Romans 12:1 and read it once again. You may remember we already examined this particular Scripture previously.

In view of *what*, are we to offer ourselves as living sacrifices?

_____

We offer ourselves to God, submitting to Him, because of His mercy and grace towards us. He has already treated us so much better than we deserve, calling us sons and daughters, and loving us unconditionally. 1 John 3:16a says, "This is how we know what love is: Jesus Christ laid down his life for us" (NIV). If He has already laid down His life, proving, once and for all, His complete love, then shouldn't we be willing to lay down our lives for Him? Like Ruth, we can proclaim with boldness "I am your servant" (Ruth 3:9 NIV) because if there is anyone that has proven Himself worthy of our trust, it's Jesus.

In the second half of verse 9, what does Ruth ask of Boaz?

_____

_____

> She is invoking him to take up his responsibility, as her redeemer, to protect her, to keep her safe, and give her a hope and a future. The dictionary's definition of redeem is simply to buy back or pay off; to clear as payment.

As we continue to read in chapter 4, this is exactly what Boaz does. The job of Ruth's redeemer, or *goel* as it was called by the ancient Israelites, was to buy back the land once belonging to Elimelech, now belonging to Naomi, and to marry the widow left behind to ensure that the family name is carried on to the next generations. In other words, to preserve and protect the livelihood of the family. "He will cover you with his feathers. He will shelter you with his wings. His faithful promises are your armor and protection" (Psalm 91:4 NLT).

Reading 2 Corinthians 5:17–21, how did God provide our ultimate protection and shelter through Jesus, the culmination of all His promises?

_____

_____

Praise be to Jesus, our One and True Redeemer. And praise be to God the Father, who "put the wrong on him who never did anything wrong, so we could be put right with God" (1 Corinthians 5:21 MSG). He bought us back. He gave us life both new and everlasting. And He gave us a hope and a future.

Let's close today by answering the following questions for reflection:

1) Have you ever submitted yourself to God? Has this ever been or does it now seem troubling or difficult for you to do? Why?

_____

_____

_____

_____

_____

_____

2) Do you believe that God is worthy of your trust and your life?

_____

_____

_____

_____

_____

_____

3) What strikes you most about the passage in 2 Corinthians I had you read?

_____

_____

_____

4) How can you be "Christ's ambassador" living out the message of reconciliation in your daily life?

_____

_____

_____

_____

_____

_____

Day Five

EMPTY TO FULL

God can do anything, you know—far more than you could ever imagine or guess or request in your wildest dreams! (Ephesians 3:20 msg).

Ruth 3 leaves us a little in suspense, doesn't it? Ruth has just laid her heart on the line by petitioning Boaz to step in as her redeemer. What you might not know or interpret from the text directly is that Boaz is somewhat surprised by her request. He is older than Ruth, possibly much older. She is not only younger than he, but also beautiful. He is flattered and overjoyed by her pursuit, but surprised, nonetheless. He agrees to become her redeemer, but there is something that must be done if he is going to do it right. True to his character, Boaz takes care of this detail first. There is one in line before him to become Ruth's kinsman redeemer and he knows he must consult with him before he proceeds. Naomi encourages her daughter-in-law to wait, to bide her time and be patient, and to see how it all turns out. She knows the character of Boaz and that he will not waste any time settling the matter. In fact, she believes he will accomplish it that very day. I wonder how long that seemingly short time period must have seemed for Ruth. Perhaps minutes felt like hours and hours like days. Time can move so slowly when your future with the man you love hangs in the balance. Lucky for us, we have the conclusion to our story in chapter 4. Take some time to read it and see what happens.

Oh, I do love a happy ending, don't you? The kinsman first in line, upon understanding the full latitude of the job, concedes redeemer responsibilities to Boaz. And not too long after that, Boaz and Ruth receive the blessing from the elders in the community. They can unite their lives together in marriage. First comes love, then comes marriage, then comes the baby in the baby carriage. That old saying holds true in this story, doesn't it? We are told that they do marry and that a baby follows soon thereafter. Ruth, once alone, a widow and a foreigner in a country not her own, has now found a partner. She is married to a man with whom she can share her life. Not only that, but she soon welcomes one of the greatest gifts ever—a child to call her own. No one is more blessed and overjoyed than sweet Naomi. Let's take a moment to recall her journey. Look back at chapter 1 and make a list of some of the adjectives used to describe her there.

_____

_____

If you remember from our first day of study this week, Naomi returned to her home country of Bethlehem to be greeted by a group of women. These women, once considered her closest friends, barely recognized her features, worn and fatigued as they are. Years of stress and sadness had embedded wrinkles in her once taut and youthful skin. Now some of those very same women have a different tune to sing. Read Ruth 4:14–15 and fill in the blanks. "Blessed be the Lord, who has not left you this day with our redeemer, and may his name be _____ in all of Israel. He shall be to you a _____ of life and a _____ of your old age…" (ESV).

Life has come full circle for Naomi. She had gone away from her home country full, but returned to it empty in deep pain. We see Naomi's pain is the kind that leaves one feeling trapped in an inescapable pit of torment and agony. But the God she serves, proves Himself faithful once again. He is a God that not only redeems, not only pays back what is owed, but heaps on blessing after blessing. He delivers fulfillment exceedingly beyond what we ever imagined we could possibly feel. Can't you just imagine Naomi rocking her sweet little grandson in her arms? In the quiet of the moment, she sings him sweet lullabies, staring into his eyes as he stares right back at her, her heart undoubtedly overflowing with joy. God has breathed new life into her tired bones with the gift of this precious gift nestled in her arms. She has been given a second chance, a reason to hope again, and a gift so abundantly good it was beyond comprehension. The good news for us is that God, the God of Naomi and Ruth, is our God also. He is the One, the only One, able to do "immeasurably more than all we ask or imagine" (Ephesians 3:20 NIV). Have you ever felt like Naomi? Have you ever cried to God from the pit? Have you wondered, as you lay your head down at night, if you will have the will in the morning to rise out of bed? Just know, dear ones, that I am praying the exceptionally powerful prayer Paul prayed over the Ephesians, over you. It goes something like this:

My response is to get down on my knees before the Father, this magnificent Father who parcels out all heaven and earth. I ask him to strengthen you by his Spirit—not a brute strength but a glorious inner strength—that Christ will live in you as you open the door and invite him in. And I ask him that with both feet planted firmly on love, you'll be able to take in with all followers of Jesus the extravagant dimensions of Christ's love. Reach out and experience the breadth! Test its length! Plumb the depths! Rise to the heights! Live full lives, full in the fullness of God. God can do anything, you know—far more than you could ever imagine or guess or request in your wildest dreams! He does it not by pushing us around but by working within us, his Spirit deeply and gently within us. Glory to God in the church! Glory to God in the Messiah, in Jesus! Glory down all the generations! Glory through all millennia! Oh, yes! (Ephesians 3:14–21 MSG).

Our God has blessed us tremendously. Even in our darkest days we can take comfort in knowing that He has blessed us with "every spiritual blessing in Christ," (Ephesians 1:3 NIV). As we close this week, I can think of no better way than counting those blessings. Open to Ephesians 1:13–14 and list every single one of the beautiful blessings that you can find. As you write, take a moment to thank Him and to offer your gratitude to the One who saves us all—the One who did for us what we cannot and could not do for ourselves. Oh, how great His mercy, love, and grace is towards us.

_____

_____

_____

_____

I am thankful for you. And for our journey together so far. I pray that you, through His love and grace, might find yourselves full again, like our sister Naomi.

Video Session Five
REDEEMED

INTRODUCTION

Ruth 2:10 says, "At this, she bowed to the ground with her face to the found. She exclaimed, 'Why have I found such favor in your eyes that you _____ me—a foreigner?'" (NIV).

In the King James Version, the word for notice is _____

_____.

The word for knowledge in the Hebrew language is nakor and it means to know, to regard, to _____ , to understand, and to recognize/pay attention.

Scripture	A God That Takes Notice	A God That Acts
Genesis 3:9,21		
Genesis 16:7,13		
Exodus 2:25		
1 Samuel 1:19–20		
Mark 5:27–29		

KINSMAN REDEEMER—GOEL

Leviticus 25:25 says, "If your brother becomes poor and sells part of his property, then his nearest redeemer shall come and _____ what his brother has sold" (ESV).

We see there are four characteristics that a *goel* has to possess in order to carry out their duties:

1) He has to be closest of kin, meaning the closest relative that is alive.

2) He must be able to redeem. Meaning he must be free of debt or need for
   _____ himself.

3) He must be willing to redeem.

4) Redemption was only complete when the price was _____
   paid.

How does Jesus fulfill each of these requirements according to the verses below?

John 3:16 _____

_____

1 John 3:5 _____

_____

John 10:18 _____

_____

John 8:36 _____

_____

What does this mean for me?

_____

_____

_____

_____

_____

EPITHET: URIAH'S WIFE

[ep-*uh*-thet]

noun

1.
any word or phrase applied to a person or thing to describe an actual or attributed quality.[1]

---

1 "Epithet," dictionary.com, accessed July 11, 2015, http://dictionary.reference.com.

Day One

IN STEP

Since we live by the Spirit, let us keep in step with the Spirit (Galatians 5:25 NIV).

Welcome back. If you are reading this, then you have survived the first four weeks of this study. For your diligence and commitment to the journey, I applaud you. I know it's not an easy task to allow God to part the seas of life's busyness and walk the hard path of trusting Him amid the chaos of this world. Whether you have done every day of homework or just a few or whether you have attended Bible study once, twice, or every week, I commend you. You have opened your heart to the living God and that is always a beautiful thing. I pray that He gives you the strength you need for today, eyes to see, and ears to hear His Spirit at work in your midst. And mostly, I pray that you would partake of the manna, the daily bread, which He faithfully provides. His daily bread arrives in all sorts of forms with the freshness of the morning. It is delivered to us in the most surprising of packages.

We continue our study of these great women in Jesus's genealogy by looking at the wife of Uriah—a woman who often remains nameless. Nameless, not to belittle or discredit her influence, but for the sole purpose of inviting us further into the warm embrace of God's grace. If you know her story, you know, that as a result of one thoughtless and impulsive choice, her name will forever be tied to a man many of us have heard of before, David. As we examine her story, we must also enter into his. I believe that their stories will speak to our own in deep and profound ways.

I live in Scottsdale, Arizona. In the summer, we swim. We swim, because when it's 115 degrees outside, that's all there really is to do. Recently, we had some of our closest friends over for dinner and an evening swim. We watched and swam alongside our kids. The kids, splashing and giggling, doing tricks off our diving board, and spilling and bubbling forth joy, breathed life into our literally dried-up bones. My fourteen-month-old daughter's favorite activity is to walk around the pool overseeing her three brothers. I followed her keeping a careful and close watch. My job was simple: to ensure that her footing was secure. I turned, for just a moment, to talk to my girlfriend and in those few seconds that my back was angled away, my daughter fell and plunged into the deep end. Then, as if a button had been pressed on a remote control, every movement became to me as if in slow motion. My attention shifted to my husband, who was sitting eight feet away from her on the ledge of the pool. I screamed, "Michael, Michael, get her!" He stared back at me in confusion, unaware of what has just happened. It had only been a few seconds, but it seemed like minutes to me. "How could he not have known what I was screaming about?" I wondered. I caught the eye of my daughter under the water, calling out in silent panic. I stood frozen in terror. My muscles were unable to move. I was like a statue and fear was the glue holding me in place. She was sinking further and further down. Then, I heard the sound of a splash. The next thing I knew she was in my arms. My girlfriend had rescued her. I drew my little girl in close. She breathed. I breathed—a tremendous sigh of relief. Thankfully, there was no water in her lungs, and after a brief moment of cuddling, she was off again. It seemed she was not even fazed by the events that had just unfolded. However, I did not so quickly forget, My hands shook and my mouth spewed words of gratitude for my friend's actions. I had let fear control me and I vowed then and there that I would never allow it to happen again.

I can relate to David a bit, as I read his story. It's like a mother watching her child sink in slow motion away from the surface and into the abyss of the deep end. As the story unfolds, David falls further and further away from His Father. One poor choice gives way to another. His soul tormented by unrest, seeking solace in all the wrong places, and ultimately sinking under the weight of his sin. Turn to 2 Samuel 11 and read the first verse. Fill in the blank. "However, David stayed _____ in Jerusalem" (2 Samuel 11:1 NLT).

The passage begins describing a time when the final remaining snow had melted giving way to spring. Spring marked the proper time for war to begin again. It was a universally accepted principle, the Scriptures tell us, for any and all kings to return to the battlefield. But King David remained behind. That evening at the pool, I followed my daughter with my senses heightened to the task at hand. I moved *with* her. But, in the blink of an eye, my position shifted, my posture altered, and I was a step behind. It happens quickly, doesn't it? We're under the watchful eye of our Father, moving in step with His Spirit, and then before we know it, we're falling a step behind.

David stays behind. This is the setup. What unfolds next isn't pretty.

Can you recall a time in your life when you fell out of step? Perhaps, now in hindsight, you see clearly how that one misstep was the catalyst for the events that followed.

_____

In light of what we have just discussed, what does Galatians 5:25 encourage us to do?

_____

Now the story continues to unfold. The first part of 2 Samuel 11:2 says, "Late one afternoon, after his midday rest, David got out of bed and was _____ on the roof of the palace" (NLT).

This word *walking* in its original language implies that David wasn't just out for a leisurely walk; he was pacing.[1]

Call to mind a time that you found yourself pacing. Reflect on the emotions flowing through your veins at that particular moment and write what comes to mind below.

_____

_____

Uncomfortable, uneasy, and stressed were the words that came to my mind. I get the sense that David is pacing because he recognizes something is not quite right. Something is off. He is out of step, or out of alignment in some way. There is somewhere he is supposed to be, and he knows it. His soul is in discord. He is discontented,

---

1 Guzik, David, "Verse by Verse Commentary 2 Samuel" (Santa Barbara, California Enduring Word Media, 2012).

and instead of seeking after His God, he takes the easy way out, and lunges for what is right in front of him. "As he looked out over the city, he noticed a woman of unusual beauty taking a bath" (2 Samuel 11:2b NLT)

What do you reach out for to quell your restless soul? The intangible or the tangible? If you would, elaborate.

_____

_____

Keep reading. "He _____ someone to find out who she was…" (2 Samuel 11:3 NLT).

He still has a choice at this point. He can stay in what I'd like to call, the noticing moment. He can avoid the temptation by acquiescing the pursuit or choosing the path of inaction. But he doesn't, does he? He sends someone to inquire after her.

Can you identify with David? Have you every moved out of a "noticing" moment when you knew you shouldn't have? Have you ever, despite hard evidence to the contrary, gone after something that wasn't yours for the taking?

> Bathsheba was from a notable and noble family. She was the daughter of Eliam. Eliam was a man who had served under David as one of David's trusted men (2 Samuel 23:34). Bathsheba was also the wife of Uriah, one of David's mighty men (2 Samuel 23:8). Perhaps Uriah was a man who had fought alongside David in the battlefield, his loyalty tested and proven worthy under the most dire of circumstances. David was told explicitly who the woman he saw bathing was. He's handed clear evidence that this pursuit would not be the right one. God might as well have been whispering in his ear, "Don't do it, David. There's a lot at stake here. More than you even know. Just say no." Tragically, David ignores the warning. Read verses 4 and 5.

I don't know how it all went down. Unfortunately, the Bible doesn't come with specifics on this. There are times I wish it did provide more details about certain things. Did Bathsheba come to him because they had some kind of previous encounter? Did she come because the electric attraction that drew him to her was reciprocated? Or did she know that to say no to the king was a death sentence? Did she come and give herself to him because she had no other choice? Was she raped that day? We can't be sure of the details, but I do know that this could have all been prevented. I do know that, although thankfully my daughter was just fine, her terrifying fall into the pool could have been avoided. When it really comes down to it, I am at fault. I'm the one who allowed her to develop this dangerous habit of toddling close to the edge of the pool. Reflecting back, I know I should never have let her get so far from the safety of my arms as we moved together that day.

Read 1 Samuel 25:42–43. How many wives does David take?

_____

David already had more than just one wife. He had already ignored God's words to him on this subject matter. He had already allowed his eyes to wander and lead him astray. So, it's true in more than one way, that David was a step behind. He had left the safety of His Master's arms and ignored God's words of caution. That day on the roof of the palace, while looking out over the city, David entered into a great temptation. He saw her, he wanted her, he went after her, and he made her his own. Let's learn from David. Before we close today, let's ask ourselves one final and painfully honest question. Are there habits developing in you today that could lead to regrets later?

_____

_____

What steps can you take right now to remove these habits? How can you allow God to replace these old ways with His ways?

_____

_____

_____

TWO WORDS THAT CHANGED EVERYTHING

When I kept silent, my bones wasted away through my groaning all day long. For day and night your hand was heavy upon me; my strength was sapped as in the heat of summer. Selah (Psalm 32:3–4 ESV).

She sat alone and completely still. The sun streamed in from the window and illuminated her stunning features. It had been four weeks since her sojourn to the palace. Two weeks of waiting. Long hours passing slowly. Lots of holding her breath. Each day bringing the sunrise and birthing just the smallest sliver of hope. "There's still a chance," she might have thought. As the sun waved good-bye and the final rays of light disappeared giving way to the darkness each night, her soul ached with the realization of the inevitable.

She sat at the kitchen table, alone. Staring across at the empty chair, a chair that belonged to her husband. Just looking at the chair sent her into an emotional tailspin and filled her with agony, betrayal, regret, and gut-wrenching shame. Tears streamed down her face, falling on the paper below. She lifted her hand, quill held prostrate. Searching for the words that wouldn't come. She knew once the letter was written and once the ink had stained the clean white scroll, her fate would be sealed. She was more like that scroll would be than she wanted to admit: stained, marked, and forever scared. She'd thought of every way to begin, searching deep into the archives of her mind for every fanciful word she could uncover, but in the end, nothing could distract, nothing could shield her from the truth. She wiped her tears and breathed in a sigh of great resolve. Pen to paper. There were only four words necessary, anything else was excess. "I am with child."

It was out now. For a moment the weight lifted. Those four little words, for centuries before and for centuries after, would change the lives of many a woman, and she was no exception. For Bathsheba and for David, as well, nothing would ever be the same.

I don't know if this is how Bathsheba felt. As I mentioned in the previous lesson, there are many details left out of the stories we find in the ancient Scriptures, but sometimes I like to, even for a moment, imagine myself in the middle of a story. It's an exercise that forces me to stop viewing biblical characters as wooden and emotionless and start picturing them as friends, maybe even best friends—the kind of friends you share your secrets with. The kind who can relate to experiencing the very same emotions that pulse through me today.

The words that we find at the end of 2 Samuel 11: 5 really do change everything. Read Leviticus 20:10 to find out just what was at stake for these two. Write your findings below:

_____

_____

For David and Bathsheba, those words, "I am with child," (2 Samuel 11:5 KJV) were a death sentence. Well, perhaps not for the king, but for Uriah's wife, they certainly spelt the end of her life.

Perhaps this gives us insight into why David, a man after God's own heart (1 Samuel 13:14), does what he is about to do in today's reading. Take a moment and read 2 Samuel 11:6–27.

I must have been six or seven. Young enough that I don't remember with detail, but old enough to recall the feeling of horror that washed over me when I realized what I had done. I do know I had asked my mom if I could color at her worktable. For as long as I can remember my mother had a space where she would create, craft, sew, etc. On that particular evening, I had my heart set on drawing and coloring with markers at *her* table. No other place would do. She agreed, under the condition that I would be extremely careful to keep the markers from bleeding onto the fabric strewn out across the table, perfectly pinned, pressed, and ready to be sewn. I was careful. Until I accidentally colored a small, a very small line of blue, across the floral patterned draperies. I froze in horror. "What am I going to do?" I remember thinking. I couldn't tell her what had happened, especially since she had told me specifically not to get marker on her fabric. I glanced up, checked to see if anyone was looking, and carefully folded the fabric back on itself just enough to cover over the marking. It was a tiny line so I'm pretty sure she never noticed. If she did, she never told me. The point is that my first response was to cover it up. That's what we do. The bigger the infraction the more of a challenge it is to cover it up.

Let's make a list of all of the schemes David devises to hide his indiscretion and keep his wrongdoings a secret. It's quite the elaborate cover-up.

_____

_____

It's easy to criticize David, to point an accusing finger in his direction, and shake our heads in disappointment and disbelief. The truth is, we all have a story. Maybe yours is similar to mine. Maybe it's something that you did as a child, when the stakes were low and nothing too devastating was on the line. Or maybe you, much like David, found yourself in a predicament much bigger than you ever imagined. Perhaps, buried under the weight of your shame, you made some choices you will regret until the day you die. There may even be some of you reading this right now who are in the middle of the muddle. Drowning, but unable to call out for help. Convinced that you must suffer alone, rather than come out from under your covering and face the consequences. I know it's hard. Like Bathsheba, I encourage you to pick up your pen and do the exceptionally hard work of getting it out on paper. Maybe two words is all you can do today. I guarantee that getting the words out on a page will somehow ease the burden you feel in your soul.

_____

_____

_____

_____

What is particularly fascinating about the end of this chapter is that David has bought into the lie. He genuinely believes he has gotten away with it. For him, it's business as usual. He moves Bathsheba into his home, takes her as his wife, and welcomes his son. I don't know how much time passes, but, for those days and months, he lives a seemingly normal life. Perhaps, he is even distracted enough by the precious bundle of joy that has arrived to forget about his own guilt and shame. For a time, he has indeed gotten away with it. On top of that, to the people living within his kingdom, he looks much less like a sinner and more like a saint. Rescuing a poor widow who was with child, caring for her, and making her a queen. The final sentence of the chapter tells a different story. It says, "But the Lord was displeased with what David had done" (2 Samuel 11:27 NLT).

> David might have fooled himself, but he hadn't fooled God. We might be able to hide from others, maybe even conceal the truth from those closest to us, but the Scriptures remind us, "People look at the outward appearance, but the Lord looks at the heart" (1 Samuel 16:7 NIV). God looks at our hearts, and it is with our hearts that He is most concerned.

Turn to Psalm 32:3–4. How does David describe his emotional state in these two verses? Have you ever felt this way? If so, describe.

_____

_____

_____

Often, we think it is God's wrath that causes us to feel the way David describes. The truth is, it's the opposite. God's deep and impenetrable concern for our hearts is why, at times, His hand can feel heavy upon us. Read Romans 2:4. What does this verse say about repentance?

_____

_____

Tomorrow we will read more about David's journey towards repentance. As we close today, let's pray. Perhaps you need to praise God for the ways He has been the ever-merciful Caretaker of your heart. Maybe it's because of His kindness that you are in the place you are in your life today, or maybe you need to confess. Leave it all at the altar of His throne, knowing that His grace casts a larger net than any of us could ever fathom. My dear sisters, He will always catch you. Whatever God is doing in your life, take a moment and allow Him to do it. It is always worth opening our hearts and allowing Him free access to our deepest of secrets. He alone is able to bring light to the darkest of places buried within our souls.

Day Three

THE POLLUTION OF INGRATITUDE

For the Lord God is a sun and shield; the Lord bestows favor and honor; no good thing does he withhold from those whose walk is blameless (Psalm 84:11 NIV).

Yesterday's study was tough. Did you feel that, or was it just me? Perhaps reading David's story illuminated your life journey in ways you weren't expecting or anticipating. Have you ever walked out of a dark movie theatre in the middle of the day, your eyes meeting with the sun's rays for the first time in hours, and felt uncomfortable? The warmth of the sun striking your back, after emerging from the air-conditioned theatre feels good, but the sun's glare on your eyes feels abrasive. We may have a similar experience when conviction melts our excuses and we are left with nowhere to hide. When there is no creative covering in sight to distract us, nor others, from the shame and guilt, we must face it. It's a difficult reality to be struck with, and one that David experiences in our reading today.

If you are feeling at all discouraged or disheartened, as we begin today, I believe that the first five words of 1 Samuel 12:1 will give you the encouragement you need. Our God is good. All. The. Time. Even when we are not.

Begin reading 2 Samuel 12:1 and pause to fill in the blanks. "_____ the Lord _____ Nathan…" (NLT)

> Have you ever felt like you were too far gone? Like you sensed you were headed down a path of destruction and ruin, but you not only continued to walk, you ran, and you could not stop? Have you ever felt as though the sins of your past, or even your present, were so great and so heinous that God surely had turned His back on you in disgust? David was an adulterer and a murderer. Yet, God sent Nathan. Don't miss this. God continues to pursue David. David has ignored God's voice, neglected to heed His warnings, and has run in the other direction, but that doesn't deter God. He remains steadfast and committed in His pursuit of His child.

Our dog is part beagle and part pug. She is a wonderful dog. Considering we brought her into our home before we had any of our children, she is lovely to them and has never lashed out, despite the pulling of her tail or the many attempts to ride her like a horse she's experienced. She is smart and sweet natured, but when it comes to food, she is obsessive, single-minded, and utterly focused. I guess it's the beagle in her, but she'll track a single grain of rice with an uncanny amount of concentration and effort. God is the ultimate tracker. You might feel like He has let you out of his sight, but He's keenly aware of every step you take and never gives up the hunt. It's why Jesus told many a story about a God that goes after the one that was lost or left behind. Whether it be a sheep, a coin, or a son (Luke 15), God is not satisfied until every last one is accounted for. If you are feeling lost today, know that you are never lost to Him.

As we continue, let me pose a question: are you a parent or have you ever been a child at one time or another? That should cover everyone! I am quite sure that at some point you have issued your child a verbal word of caution or received one yourself. Perhaps there were even several words of caution. Just maybe that word of caution was tuned out. Maybe your child or your child-self pretended not to hear, or in a moment of complete disobedience, ignored the parental advice outright. What happened next? Did either you or your parent take the next step, grab hold of an arm firmly, pull a body close, and with a quiet, but calculated tone, say, "If you do that again, there are going to be some serious issues"? God sends Nathan to provide this firm reprimand to David because nothing else seems to be working. Read Hebrews 12:5–11.

Why does God discipline?

_____

_____

What makes us legitimate children of God?

_____

_____

What does God's discipline produce in us?

_____

_____

As we continue to read David's story, let's remember that God's discipline towards him, and towards us, is actually good news. It is one of the many ways He proves His love for us. Let's move forward by reading 2 Samuel 12:2–9.

So far, our story has been building, and the tension rising. It reaches its moment of climax when, after David's anger burns towards the rich man, Nathan cries out, "You are *that* man!" (2 Samuel 12:7 NLT). Nathan lets David know without any question that he is to blame. David is now faced with a choice. He can own up to what he has done or continue to live in ignorance.

I absolutely love what Nathan, speaking on God's behalf, says next, "I anointed you king of Israel and saved you from the power of Saul. I gave you your master's house and his wives and the kingdoms of Israel and Judah. And if that had not been enough, I would have given you much, much more" (2 Samuel 12:7–8 NLT).

God is most concerned with our total healing. You and I would think that the greatest of the sins committed by David were adultery and murder. Those acts were the aftermath of the much larger and more pollutant issue. God aims His attention at the heart of the matter. Somewhere along the line, David had become ungrateful. Clouded by his ingratitude, he believes Uriah's wife to be the solution to his discontented soul. All he really needed was a bended knee, a posture of gratitude, and a heart fully satisfied with the good gifts he had already received and those continuing to be bestowed on him.

When you and I live with a "grass is always greener on the other side" mentality, we will always fall devastatingly short of the full life that Jesus came to give us. In John 10, Jesus warned of a thief who would come to kill and destroy. That thief comes in many disguises. Perhaps the most damaging and effective is ingratitude. As soon as we buy into the bold-faced lie that we are entitled to more than we have been given, we have lost a critical battle being waged over our souls.

The truth, and it's a difficult one, is that we deserve death. We've earned a life separated from the God who made us and formed us in our mother's wombs. Instead of death, we are given grace. We are made one with our God by the power of Jesus Christ through His sacrifice on the cross. We are forever reunited with the only One who can makes us whole. This is not what we deserve. It's the scandal of grace. It's a God who freely gives us what we have not earned. How many times do we continually believe that we deserve more? Or that we've earned more? For many of us, there's always a nagging craving and a yearning for more that refuses to be subdued.

Ann Voscamp puts it this way, "We only enter into the full life if our faith gives thanks. Because how else do we accept His free gift of salvation if not with thanksgiving? Thanksgiving? Thanksgiving is the evidence of our acceptance of what He gives. Thanksgiving is the manifestation of our yes! to His grace. Thanksgiving is inherent to a true salvation experience; thanksgiving is necessary to live the well, whole fullest life."[1]

How do we combat ingratitude and the toxicity it inevitably causes? We choose to be thankful. When I have to clean the pee-stained toilets, I am thankful for running water.

When my child throws up in the middle of the night all over his or her sheets, I am thankful for a washing machine and the medicine I have to give them. When I lose my

---

1 Voscamp, Ann, One Thousand Gifts (Grand Rapids, Michigan, Zondervan, 2010), 39.

job, I am thankful for the money I have in my savings, and a community around me to love and support me through a difficult time. When I get a flat tire, I am thankful for AAA. When there is a death in my family, I am thankful for the messages of love I receive from friends. When all there is to eat in my fridge is eggs and only one lone can of peanut butter in my pantry, I am thankful I have food at all. When life is hard, I am thankful for a God that never leaves nor forsakes me.

> There is always something to be thankful for. If our hearts are not in the practice of seeking gratefulness, though, we will miss the blessings bestowed on us. I wonder, I really wonder, how things could have been different, if, when David was on the rooftop, he would have looked out over the city and recalled to mind all the ways in which God had been faithful to Him. If he had been thinking about all the good gifts he had received, I wonder if he would have even noticed Bathsheba. We won't ever know for certain, but I bet the answer would be no.

As always, we will close with some questions for personal reflection. As usual, they are not easy. Once again, I encourage you to be as honest as you possibly can.

Read Psalm 84:11. Do you believe that God does not withhold any good thing from us?

_____

Read Romans 8:32. What does this Scripture tell us to be thankful for?

_____

In what ways, if any, is your heart ungrateful?

_____

_____

Is there something in particular you feel you are entitled to have that you have not received? Is there a relationship that you have felt entitled to have that has not been reciprocated? Has this sense of entitlement, in either case, led you to make any choices you regret?

_____

_____

_____

Is your life characterized by ingratitude or gratitude?

_____

_____

_____

Take a moment to make a list of the things you are grateful for. Try to be specific in light of your experiences in this particular moment in which you find yourself.

_____

_____

_____

_____

_____

_____

Day Four

REAPING WHAT WE SOW

You were taught, with regard to your former way of life to put off your old self, which is being corrupted by its deceitful desires, to be made new in the attitude of your minds; and to put on the new self, created to be like God in true righteousness and holiness (Ephesians 4:22–24 NIV).

Thus far in our study of David, we've learned more about what *not* to do, than what *to do*. As the phrase goes, "Do what I say, not what I do." Today David redeems himself. He is far from perfect; it's not too difficult to arrive at that conclusion. That said, what he does with his imperfection demands our respect and attention.

I don't know about you, but "I'm sorry" can be the hardest two words to say in the English language. I'm not sure there is one person who takes pleasure in letting this little phrase roll off their tongues or who honestly enjoys admitting their wrongs. It's just not who we are. The truth is nothing can be more of a catalyst for positive change than a heartfelt apology—one in which we sacrifice our dignity on the altar of unadulterated vulnerability. This, my dear sisters, is exactly what David does.

Let's skip over a few verses. We will return to them shortly. Read 2 Samuel 12:13, and fill in the blanks. "Then David _____ to Nathan, "I have sinned against the _____" (2 Samuel 12:13a NLT).

No excuses. No justifications. He just comes right out and says it he was wrong. He realizes there is no one he's hurt more than God Himself. You have to admire the guy.

For most of us there's always a "but" involved. We might say or think "I'm sorry, but I'd really rather not bear the full load of fault. I'd rather distribute it on others I feel deserve some amount of blame, even if I know deep down that the only real person at fault is me, myself, and I."

Can you identify? Do you ever find it hard to say, "I'm sorry"? Is there a specific instance that comes to your mind?

_____

_____

_____

Take a moment and turn to Psalm 51. You'll never read a more heartfelt apology than the one penned by David here. Read through it and answer the following question. Are there any verses in particular that stand out to you? How so?

_____

_____

_____

Fill in the following blank from the remainder of verse 13. Nathan replied, "Yes, but the Lord has _____ you, and you won't die for this sin" (2 Samuel 12:13b NLT).

As quickly as David is to admit wrong, God is even quicker to forgive. Numbers 14:18 tells us, "The Lord is slow to anger, abounding in love, and forgiving sin and rebellion" (NIV). David deserved death under the Law, but God, who is merciful, spared him of that punishment. Of course, there is more to the Scripture I referenced above than what I originally let on. Turn to chapter 14 of Numbers and finish verse 18. What does it say?

_____

_____

> Keep this Scripture in mind as we move on to our next reading. I think you will quickly observe how it applies. Look at 2 Samuel 12:14–19.

I enjoy reading about God's grace, love, and mercy, but when I get to the part where we have to come face-to-face with our guilt and deal with the consequences of our wrongdoings, well, I sometimes wish I could skip over those parts. This next portion of David's story, the section where God afflicts the child that Bathsheba bears with a deadly disease, isn't my favorite. The bottom line is that when we choose to ignore the voice of God and to move away from Him instead of towards Him, bad stuff happens. In David and Bathsheba's case, we don't really know how it all went down. Some commentators assert that it was God Himself who struck the baby with illness. Others argue, that this was a natural consequence of David's disobedience. 1

One of my Dad's favorite phrases when I was growing up was, "Sometimes bad things happen." I hated it when he pulled this phrase out and used it on me. Even now, the sound of those particular words strung together make me cringe a little. What I can see now is that the phrase should go something like this, "Sometimes bad things happen when you choose your own way instead of God's." Whether we like it or not, just as the text asserts, our choices affect future generations for better or worse. It's why history repeats itself. Don't get me wrong, it is possible to alter the course of our family's emotional and spiritual DNA, but it takes a conscious effort and the Spirit of God to effect lasting change. You may remember this was one of the themes in our first week. There were some very unfortunate events that occurred, not only in the life of David, but in the lives of his sons and daughters. Most of them are tied in some way to David's affair with Bathsheba.

Look up the following Scriptures and make a list of the consequences of David's sin.

---

1 Guzik, David, "Verse by Verse Commentary 2 Samuel" Kindle Edition (Santa Barbara, California Enduring Word Media, 2012).

2 Samuel 11:5

_____

_____

2 Samuel 11:21

_____

_____

2 Samuel 12:18

_____

_____

2 Samuel 13:1–14

_____

_____

2 Samuel 13:22–29

_____

_____

2 Samuel 18:1–14

_____

_____

1 Kings 11:3

_____

_____

It isn't pretty. In fact, this list is altogether devastating. An unwanted pregnancy, a man murdered, a dead baby, David's daughter raped by his own son, a son murdered another, a son who fought his own father leading the country to civil war, and another son with a wandering eye to name a few.

I didn't have you read all this to discourage you. As we learned yesterday, sometimes the weight of sin—our own sin—upon our shoulders seems too much to bear. Never mind the actuality of its ripple effect on those we care most about. Facing this might be good for some of us, especially me, who need to have a little bit of healthy fear. Perhaps a better way of saying it is that we should allow the story of David to make us keenly and cautiously aware. Let's think about the ramifications our decisions might have, not only on our future, but our children's and our children's children's futures as well.

As we near the end of today's lesson, let's end on a good note. Read 2 Samuel 12:20–25.

How does David reply when asked by his advisors why he has stopped his mourning?

_____

_____

_____

How should David's response speak to how we should move forward from our past sins?

_____

_____

_____

_____

David asked, "But why should I fast when he is dead?" (2 Samuel 12:23 NLT). He could have sulked. He could have drowned in his own self-pity. He could have waded in the pool of self-loathing and dove head first into the sea self-hatred. It certainly would have been easy to do so, but he understood an important truth: what's done was done. There was nothing he could do in the present to change what happened in the past. The only way to move on was to let go. God had forgiven him. All that was left was to allow himself that same amount of forgiveness.

Ephesians 4:22–24 says this: "You were taught, with regard to your former way of life, to put off your old self, which is being corrupted by its sinful desires, to be made new in the attitude of your minds; and to put on the new self, created to be like God in true righteousness and holiness" (NLT).

Is there anything in your life you need to forgive yourself for?

_____

_____

How can you walk in your "new self" today?

_____

_____

_____

As we close, let's rejoice. God's love keeps no record of wrongs, and "as far as the east is from the west, so he has removed our transgressions from us" (Psalm 103:12 NIV). Not only that, but God does "…not treat us as our sins deserve or repay us according to our iniquities" (Psalm 103:10 NIV). His blessings continue to flow. David and Bathsheba do conceive again. Their son, whom the scriptures say "the Lord loved" (2 Samuel 12:24 NIV), is called Solomon. And it is Solomon, the fourth in line and the one born as a result of a sinful relationship, who God specifically appoints as the next king. Solomon becomes the wisest man to ever live before Jesus, and the one whom God calls and equips to build His temple. Solomon's role causes his dear mother, our Bathsheba, to find her way into the genealogy of Jesus the Christ. If that does not point to the grace of an ever-loving and compassionate God, I am not sure what does. I am thankful today because the God of David, of Solomon, and of Bathsheba is my God. His grace towards us is as extravagant as it was then. Let us bask in that truth.

Day Five

LEGACY

Her children arise and call her blessed… (Proverbs 31: 28 NIV).

For the last four days, we have turned our attention towards David. As I mentioned at the beginning of the week, it really is impossible to study Bathsheba without examining David. The fabric of their stories is tightly interwoven, but today, we will shift our focus to the mysterious and beautiful woman that stole David's heart. We are going to pick up with our story when David is "very old," as the text puts it, and getting ready to appoint one of his sons to the throne.

Read 1 Kings 1, taking special note of anytime you see Bathsheba's name appear. Circle it, if you are willing to write in your Bible.

We are told Nathan goes to Bathsheba in verse 11. What does he ask her to do?

_____

_____

_____

What does this say about the relationship between Bathsheba and David?

_____

_____

_____

_____

_____

Nathan, the prophet who obviously held the king's deep respect and loyalty, is the one God had sent to confront David with his sins earlier in the story. This same man, trusted by God, approaches Bathsheba with some rather troubling news in 1 Kings. Nathan believes that Bathsheba should be the one to present her son with this news. What exactly is this troubling news? Adonijah, the *son* of King David, has hijacked the throne. Hearing that your own brother is trying to overthrow you is not exactly the kind of thing you want to be told as a king. It is somewhat interesting that of all the people Nathan could have chosen to relay this message to Solomon, he picked Bathsheba. It is certainly telling of the nature of their relationship. Despite the scandal and turmoil surrounding Bathsheba's entry into the royal family, we see that she has remained committed to preserving and protecting both her husband's and her son's well-being. We get even greater insight into her character as we continue to read. Pick up with the story in 1 Kings 2:10–25.

That pesky Adonijah is relentless in his pursuit of the throne. His request to marry Abishag may seem harmless at first glance, but his motives are undoubtedly not. Abishag is one of his father's concubines. Although she is no longer bound to him, as the covenant of marriage has been broken because of David's death, to marry her would be a direct attempt to undermine the rule of Solomon. It's a trick he most likely learned from his even more menacing and unruly brother, Absalom. Glance at 2 Samuel 16:20–23 to read about the unfortunate event involving Absalom and David's concubines. Yikes.

> On a side note, while modeling our lives after David's character proves prudent in some aspects, I think this story proves that patterning our parenting style after his may not be the best choice. We see that he took little disciplinary action towards his children, which resulted in some fairly contemptuous grown men.

Why do you think Bathsheba agreed to this somewhat incredulous and inappropriate request that Nathan is pleading her to make before Solomon?

_____

_____

_____

_____

If you said it's because she has Solomon's best interests at heart, then you were right. Adonijah needed to go. He had proven himself vexing and troublesome enough. She knew that her son's life would be in danger as long as Adonijah was still breathing. So, she agreed to make this "small" request, knowing it was really a big deal. Being aware that this would rouse Solomon's anger, but compel him to take lasting and irreversible action, she spoke to him.

Although I don't condone murder or conspiracy to commit murder, you have to admire her audacity. She decided to do whatever it took to safeguard and champion her son. My favorite part of this passage, perhaps because I have three boys myself, occurs in verse 19 of 1 Kings 2. Fill in the blanks. "The king _____ from his throne to meet her, and he _____ down before her. When he sat on his throne again, the king ordered that a _____ be brought for his mother, and she sat at his right hand" (NLT).

I love it! Solomon's request to have a throne brought for his mother takes chivalry to a whole new level, doesn't it? This verse speaks volumes about the relationship between Bathsheba and her son. What can you observe about their mother-son dynamic from these verses?

_____

_____

_____

_____

_____

Read Proverbs 31:28. What does this verse say about the children of the wife of noble character outlined in this chapter?

_____

_____

_____

"Her children arise and call her blessed" (Proverbs 31:28 NIV). This Scripture has taken on deeper meaning for me recently. Just over a month ago, my grandmother (I refer to her as Nona) lost her life to cancer. She was eighty-six and had lived a long life, but, I admit, I still felt cheated. This was a woman, who through both her direct and indirect influence over my life, undeniably, made me who I am today. So much good in me can be attributed to her influence. She loved me, cherished me, supported me, and was one of my number one cheerleaders for all thirty-one years of my life. The fact that she won't be around to do the same for my kids hurts. Her mother, my granny, had lived to be almost one hundred, and so when we found out the cancer had spread all over her body and death was imminent, I was shocked. In my mind, we still had so many good years ahead of us.

In death, in sadness, in heartache, and in anguish, God entered in. With Him came the thrill of hope, unexpected joy in the most peculiar of places, and cracked windows into His living room of grace. Nona lived in Canada, so I wasn't able to be with her in the last weeks of her life. Her husband and children—my mom, aunt, and two uncles—were by her side every single day. She miraculously felt very little pain despite the cancer's ravenous hold on her body, and I am convinced it was because of God's hand of protection upon her. He gave her, and all of the family, a gift in those final months and days. Because no heavy medications were necessary to help manage the pain, she remained in her home—in her very own bed—as she lived out her final moments here on earth. My grandfather could slip into their bed next to her and grab a hold of her hand as she drifted to sleep. Her children tucked her in and could kiss her goodnight. My uncle slept on the floor of their tiny little condo for the entirety of her last month, ensuring that there would be someone there, if necessary. They talked, told stories, monitored her pain, changed her bed sheets, and attended to her every need. She died, surrounded by the people she had loved so well. Undoubtedly, she left a legacy of love imprinted on all our hearts that will forever be remembered and cherished. I often pray, as I raise my own children, that I can carry that legacy with same amount of grace as she did. My Dad sent me a text message one night after he left my grandparent's home, describing some of what had been transpiring in my absence. It said, "One, if not the most beautiful, gracious, and touching aspects of Nona's impending departure is observing the loving and gentle manner in which her children are caring for her! This brought me to tears last night as I lay in bed recounting the past few days. God is gracious and good."

> The greatest gift you can give anyone is unconditional love. It possesses a transformational quality that nothing else can rival. It has a way of getting into the core of us and bringing about a change we didn't think possible. When we support others, champion them, defend them, protect them, encourage them, intercede for them, and pour our lives into them, we allow space for miracles to occur in our midst.

Isn't this what Jesus has done for all of us? Read Hebrews 7:22–28. This Scripture tells us that Jesus always lives to do what for us?

_____

_____

_____

_____

The Message puts it this way, "Earlier there were a lot of priests, for they died and had to be replaced. But Jesus's priesthood is permanent. He's there from now to eternity to save everyone who comes to God through him, always on the job to speak up for them" (Hebrews 7:23–25 MSG).

I love how Bathsheba speaks up for Solomon and intercedes for him, but I am grateful, even more, for how Jesus does that for us today. Always on our side and always advocating for us, the one and true Priest, who offered Himself as the sacrifice, who forever put us right with God, and who continually rains down unconditional love upon our lives, calls us to do the same for others.

How is God calling you to intercede for your loved ones or even for those you do not know?

_____

_____

_____

_____

We all want to have our children arise and call us blessed. How can we love well today so we can leave a legacy tomorrow? As you answer this question, would you participate in a small activity with me? Take some time to pray. Try for a moment or two to quiet yourself before Him and listen. Do not offer up any requests. If your mind distracts you with your to-do list, grab a scrap of paper and write those things down. Getting those things on paper will help you clear you mind and become more focused on opening up to His presence. Invite the Holy Spirit to draw your mind to the things He has for you. Ask Him if there are specific ways you can love well today, this week, and this month? Then, pay careful attention to where your mind drifts. Take comfort in this Scripture, "The Spirit searches all things, even the deep things of God. For who knows a person's thoughts except their own spirit within them? In the same way no one knows the thoughts of God except the Spirit of God…But we have the mind of Christ" (1 Corinthians 2:10–11, 16 NIV). Because of God's Spirit in us, we have the mind of Christ. Trust in that as you listen before Him today. He may very well call certain people to your mind. If so, write down their names or initials in the space below and begin by praying for them. He may even lead you to certain actions. He might be urging you to take in your specific area of influence. Whatever comes to your mind that you believe to be the Spirit's prompting, record it.

Video Session Six
STRENGTH IN WEAKNESS

INTRODUCTION

2 Samuel 12:13 says, "Then David said to Nathan, "I have sinned against the

_____ " (NIV).

DAVID'S CONFESSION

"My sacrifice, O God, is a broken spirit; a _____ and _____

heart you, God, will not despise" (Psalm 51:17 NIV).

"I learned God-worship when my _____ was shattered. Heart-shattered

lives ready for love don't for a moment escape God's notice" (Psalm 51:17 MSG).

PAUL'S THORN

A troublesome person today is commonly referred to as a "pain in the neck." In

_____ such a person was called a "barb in the eye" or a "thorn

in the side."[1]

2 Corinthians 12:9 says, "But He said to me, 'My grace is sufficient for you, my power

is made _____ in weakness'…" (NIV).

---

1 Belleville, Linda, 2 Corinthians *The IVP New Testament Commentary Series*, (Downers Grove,
Illinois 1996.)

The *IV New Testament Commentary Series* says, "God's power neither displaces weakness nor overcomes it. On the contrary, it comes to its full strength _____ _____."[1]

The word for "perfect" in the Greek is *teleios*, which means "to find _____ or be accomplished in."

The verb for "rest" in the Greek is *episkeeno,* and it means "to make one's _____ in" or to "take up one's abode in."[2]

How does weakness becomes strength in David's life?

1) _____

2) _____

3) _____

4) _____

What does this mean for me?

_____

_____

_____

_____

1 Belleville, Linda, 2 Corinthians *The IVP New Testament Commentary Series*, (Downers Grove, Illinois, InterVarsity Press. 1996.)

2 Belleville, Linda, 2 Corinthians *The IVP New Testament Commentary Series*, (Downers Grove, Illinois, InterVarsity Press. 1996.)

Week Six

RISING ACTION: MARY

noun

1.

a related series of incidents in a literary plot
that build toward the point of greatest interest.[1]

---

1 "Rising Action," dictionary.com, accessed July 12, 2015,
http://dictionary.reference.com.

Day One

MAY YOUR WORDS TO ME BE FULFILLED

The person who trusts me will not only do what I'm doing but even greater things, because I, on my way to the Father, am giving you the same work to do that I've been doing. You can count on it (John 14:12 MSG).

Today we begin the final week of our journey together. I am deeply grateful for each of you. You have given the gift of your time and the gift of an open heart and open hands; in turn, I hope you have received a new and fresh word from our God.

This morning, as I write, I am profoundly thankful for that God, whose consistent presence moves us and draws us to Himself. He enters in. His work within and through us is never finished. His story has always been tightly bound and woven into the lives of those He calls children, and Mary, our focus for this week, is the paramount example of this. This story is about a simple girl from an obscure village who received an extraordinary invitation and was a brave enough to say yes.

My prayer for you, dear ones, as we begin, is that we all find the courage to say yes to the work He desires to accomplish in and through our lives.

> Read Luke 1:26–38. For many of you, this passage will be familiar. You may have read these Scriptures in your personal time of devotion or heard them read every year in church in conjunction with the Christmas story. As you open this sacred text today, may it resonate and rest in you in a new way. May you experience the "power of the Most High" (Luke 1:35 NIV), as Mary did thousands of years ago.

We have the joy and the privilege of reading these Scriptures over two thousand years after the events took place. Sometimes reading them this far removed can be to our detriment. As I pore over these verses and all the events that transpired—from the angel's visit to Mary's pregnancy brought about by the Holy Spirit, to the actual birth of this holy child—I realize these events could quickly lose the utterly spectacular flavor they actually had. They have become too familiar, perhaps. I've lost the awe, the wonder, and the pure shock of it all. Before we go on, let's pause for a moment and really consider what it was like to be in Mary's shoes.

How do you think Mary felt when the angel appeared to her and related the astonishing news that she would be the mother of the "Son of the Most High" (Luke 1:32 NIV)? Perhaps the better question is, how would you feel and react if you were Mary in this same set of circumstances? Imagine Jesus had not yet come. You are a young girl, a virgin, and an angel appears before you with such a message. What would you think? How would you feel?

It's the most bizarre, unbelievable, stupefying, and strange story you'll ever read. But it's unrivaled in its stunning and mysterious truth and beauty. God's only Son, conceived by the Holy Spirit enters the world as an infant child born to two teenagers. It's a stunning revelation, and if you're honest with yourself, flat-out weird. In the moments I reflect on this, what I am most amazed by is how Mary responds to it all. Fill in the blanks from Luke 1:38. "'I am the _____ servant,' Mary answered, 'May your word to me be _____'" (NIV).

Sure, she has a few other reactions before this. She is "greatly troubled" (Luke 1:29 NIV), as the text points out, but her statement in verse 38 is how she ends up responding. It's impressive. Actually, it's exceptionally impressive. Verse 38 could be summed up simply with these two words, "Yes, Lord." It's hard for me to believe or understand how she could respond with this level of authentic obedience, but she does. There is a pattern of these responses in the Scriptures. They don't particularly make sense to us humans in the equation, but God, the other factor in the equation, is almost always up to something behind the scenes. Examine the following passages and note the responses of each of the characters mentioned.

Isaiah 6:1–8

_____

Genesis 22:1–3

_____

Genesis 6:11–14; 22

_____

Joshua 6:1–7

_____

Mark 1:16–18

_____

John 4: 43–50

_____

I can remember vividly a conversation I shared with my mentor while sitting in my college cafeteria. It is permanently etched in my brain. We met weekly and she poured into me, discipled me, and inspired me probably more than she knows. We were chatting about an upcoming event put on by the campus ministry (she was on staff and I was a leader) that day over lunch. We called it "The Edge" and it was InterVarsity Christian Fellowship's key outreach event held once a semester with the singular goal of attracting students who would not usually find themselves at our weekly meetings. The staff had prayed and felt led to my name. I was the one that would teach that night, they were certain of it. They felt confident of my calling, and all that was left now was for me to say yes. I was surprised and extremely honored. Before I could really think about the implications, the words shot forth from my mouth. "Yes!" I blurted, "Of course, I will do it." I turned to my mentor and added, "I'm not sure what I just got myself into." Looking back on my life up until now, I seem to put myself in these situations frequently. I say yes, and then later end up wondering, "Did I really agree to that?"

At the time, my mentor laughed when I said, "I'm not sure what I've gotten into." Then she said something that has stuck with me. She said, "You know, Christy, I think that even when it doesn't all make sense, even if you are not sure you are up for the task, even if it all seems daunting and out of your comfort zone, saying yes, in spite of all the reasons to say no, is the mark of a true disciple."

Can you recall a time in your life when you said yes in spite of your fears? Is there something you feel God is calling you to say yes to, even though the thought it is making your palms clammy?

_____

_____

"'I am the Lord's servant,' Mary answered. 'May your word to me be fulfilled'" (Luke 1:38 NIV). In spite of everything Mary got on the line here, and there's a lot on the line, she agrees to the plan. There are certainly many more reasons to say no to this mission than there are to say yes. There is a distinct possibility that the man she loves and is betrothed to may leave her because of this holy pregnancy. There will undoubtedly be a large majority of her acquaintances and even friends and family that will point fingers, snicker, and cast judgment on her behind her back. What do you possibly make of an angel of God appearing to *you,* and announcing the unbelievable and unprecedented news that you will carry God's Son? I don't know how she did it, but she said yes. In spite of it all, she proclaims, "May your word to me be fulfilled" (Luke 1:38 NIV).

Perhaps, you are wrestling with that very same question in your own journey right now. Why should I say yes, when there are far more justifiable reasons to say no? The answer is right there in our text. Write out verse 37 below.

> No word from God will ever fail. That is a promise that we can cling to, a promise for which we can risk everything. We can bet our reputation, our character, and our very lives on God, and it is always a safe bet because He will always follow through on His Word. This does not mean that our lives will be easy. We may encounter all sorts of bumps in the road. There may be moments, when in loneliness and despair, we cry out in desperation, "God, are You even there?" But rest assured, He has promised to never leave, nor forsake us, and therefore, we are never alone. How can we know this for certain? Because He has promised us that, and He cannot go back on His Word. How does Mary say yes? She understands, deep within her being, that God can be trusted—that His Word will never fail.

What is supremely beautiful about this plan Mary finds herself in the center of is that God has already been at work. He is not asking Mary to trust Him to do something He hasn't already done. Is it a coincidence that Elizabeth in her old age has conceived, and that she is a close relative of Mary's? Absolutely not. God, in His divine providence, has paved a way for Mary's belief. He knows the request He is making of Mary is extraordinary. He understands she's going to need a little nudge to propel her into what might be the greatest and most unbelievable task ever asked of any human being in history. If there is anyone who understands our fears, our limitations, and our reservations, it is the One that made us. "He is before all things," Paul writes, "and in Him all things hold together" (Colossians 1:17 NIV). God went before Mary, granting a seemingly impossible pregnancy to the aging Elizabeth to prove to Mary that He was in the business of making the impossible possible. It's as if he is saying "See, Mary, you are in extremely capable hands. Now, it's your turn."

Not only does God pave the way for Mary through her cousin's pregnancy, but He gives her something else. In verse 34, Mary asked the angel in response to everything she has just heard, "How will this be, since I am a virgin?" (Luke 1:34 ESV). What answer does the angel give to her? The angel says, "…the power of the Most High will overshadow you…" (Luke 1:35 NIV). In other words, "Mary, I got it. The how is not for you to worry about. The miracle that is about to unfold is not your responsibility to bear." If I were her, I would have let out a huge sigh of relief. There is nothing that provides more comfort from the scorching sun than shade. Mary's breath of fresh air came with the promise that the power of God Himself would shade her, protect her, and overshadow her. As it says in Psalm 121:5, "The Lord watches over you—the Lord is your shade at your right hand" (NIV). Some of you reading this are exhausted. You feel like a plant in need of water and shriveling under the sun's heat. Perhaps, you feel as though God is calling you into something far beyond what you can handle, much like Mary did. Take heart, dear sister, the One whose Word never fails, has promised to watch over you and shade you. The truth is that no matter where we find ourselves in life, we can all benefit from the words of this psalm. If you consider yourself a disciple of Christ, be warned, He has great plans for you. His dreams for you are much larger than you could dream for yourself. How do I know this? Because He told us this directly. Read John 14:12–17.

What kinds of things will the disciples do?

_____

_____

What does Jesus ask the Father to give us?

_____

If we listen, He will ask us to follow Him to uncertain and unknown places. He will ask us to say yes, even when everything in our human body demands we say no! Jesus says, "Anyone who loves me will obey my teaching…" (John 14:23 NIV). Our obedience is all He asks for. He'll take care of the rest. The question that remains for us is this: will we follow?

_____

Day Two

HE HAS DONE GREAT THINGS

*Praise the Lord, my soul; all my inmost being, praise his holy name,
Praise the Lord, my soul, and forget not all his benefits* (Psalm
103:1–2 NIV).

Let's pick up where we left off. Mary has had an angelic encounter and responded to a message from the living God. Just like any of us would have done, she ran as quickly as possible to share the news with her girlfriend, or in this case, her cousin Elizabeth. Women have a tendency to want to share less earth shattering news than that with each other, and Mary was no exception. She made her way to the home of Elizabeth and Zechariah. Read Luke 1:39–45.

What word does Elizabeth use to describe Mary on three separate occasions?

_____

_____

The word *blessed* can have different meanings for different people. What does that word mean to you?

_____

_____

_____

There are times I feel as though the hand of God literally picks me up and places me in the direct line of something good He is doing. I notice He chooses to use me to accomplish something significant in my own life or in the lives of those around me. Have you ever felt that? Something happens that is so wonderful and so beyond your expectations, that you find yourself in the middle of circumstances you could never have dreamed up yourself. A check is placed in your hands for the exact amount needed to cover your house payment for the month. Words are spoken to you by a friend at the exact moment you needed to hear them most. In the midst of moments like these, it is nearly impossible to deny that God is responsible. I must confess there are times when my first impulse is to take that thing He has done and claim it as my own. It's not pretty. It's far from humble, but it's the truth.

I am, at the very center of my nature, a people pleaser. And what do we people pleasers crave more than anything else? The praise of those whom we seek to please. When we people pleasers get that praise we long for, we ingest it and we gobble it up like we've never been on the receiving end of a compliment before. If I was Mary, and Elizabeth called me blessed over and over again, I might start thinking that the blessing must have something to do with me. Surely, this gift bestowed is a direct result of my considerably pure and chaste character. I might take that blessing and hoard it. Hi, my name is Christy, and I am a blessing hoarder.

How about you? Please tell me I'm not the only one that does this. Can you identify? Write your answer in the blank below.

_____

_____

_____

But here is the thing about that word *blessing*. By definition, a blessing comes to us as the result of someone else's actions. It is very difficult to bless yourself. Unless, of course, you are sneezing, in which case it is not only acceptable but also encouraged. A true blessing, under most circumstances, is generally given to us by an outside source. One commentary put it this way, "to be blessed is to be happy because God has touched one's life."[1] The many, varied, and extravagant gifts God showers on us from above are what constitutes blessing.

---

1   Bock, Darrell L., 2 Corinthians " *The IVP New Testament Commentary Series*, (Downers Grove, Illinois InterVarsity Press. 1994).

We've talked about blessing before and even read this particular Scripture on several different occasions. Remind yourselves of what Ephesians 1:3 says about this topic?

_____

What is the very first word in verse 3?

_____

Praise. Praise who? Praise the Lord. Mary understood the importance of deferring whatever praise was directed to her back to God. In the moments she is called blessed, she does not hoard the blessing. Instead, she pours the blessing out. She lays it at the feet of the One who blessed her first. Another way of saying it is that she gives praise in response to the blessing. She gives credit where credit is due. Read what is known as the *Magnificat* found in Luke 1:46–56. Take note of, or if you feel comfortable writing in your Bible, underline the words, "He has," each time you find them.

How many times did you notice this phrase?

_____

List all the things for which Mary credits God.

_____

_____

"From now on all generations will call me blessed" she says, "for the mighty One has done great things for me" (Luke 1:48-49 NIV). Mary understands something that I think we all should note. She recognizes that God owes her absolutely nothing. On the contrary, she owes God everything. Let's finish today by crafting our own Magnificat. Let's praise Him for all that the mighty One has done for us. There is not one of us who has not been blessed, so let's give God the credit He more than deserves.

Fill in the following blanks with the word *my*. And after each, "He has" write what He has done for you:

_____ soul glorifies the Lord and _____ spirit rejoices in God _____ Savior.

He has _____

He has _____

He has _____

He has _____

He has _____

He has _____

Lord, You have done all these things. May all honor and glory be unto You.

GREAT IS YOUR FAITHFULNESS

Yet this I call to mind and therefore I have hope: Because of the Lord's great love we are not consumed, for his compassions never fail (Lamentations 3:21 NIV).

Yesterday we spent some time blessing God in response to the numerous ways He has first blessed us. Go back to the beginning of yesterday's lesson and read what David wrote in Psalm 103. This exercise of blessing is one that we need to practice. In my experience, this exercise is not one that comes easily to us, which is why it's not totally surprising that David challenges us to not only bless the Lord, but to keep all His benefits in the forefront of our minds. He urges not to forget. This is somewhat of a recurring theme in the Psalms and throughout the Scriptures as a whole. Look up the following verses and write a brief summary in the blanks provided.

Psalm 77:11

_____

_____

Psalm 143:5

_____

_____

Psalm 105:5

_____

_____

The act of worship beckons us to look back, to recall, and to remember the great work the Lord has done. I think there is no better story that teaches us the gravity of looking back than that of Moses and the Israelites. I am sure that many of you are familiar with this story. Moses, called and appointed by God, led the Israelites out of slavery. Of course, it took ten very unpleasant plagues delivered by God Himself to convince Pharaoh to concede to the release of the Israelites. Even then, Pharaoh didn't totally get it because he sent a whole bunch of his men in pursuit of God's people, only to have each and every one of them swallowed up by the Red Sea. It's a great story, but what interests me more, especially in light of our study today, is what happens next. We find the Israelites wandering in the desert. At the first sign of struggle, they allow the nagging hunger in their bellies and their parched mouths to unhinge them completely. They cry out against the Lord. Against who? You know, God, the One that just saved them from two hundred and fifteen *years* of slavery under the Egyptians. Read what happens in Numbers 20:1–4.

Can you believe it? They actually thought it would be better back in Egypt. They are free for the first time in a long, long time, but they'd rather go back. I read in disbelief, I scoff, I judge, and I am appalled. Deep down I know the truth. I am much more like them than I would like to admit. There is something to all this talk about remembering. I wonder if the Israelites might have acted differently had they paused to remember the many ways in which God had supernaturally intervened on their behalf. I wonder how they would have felt if they had counted the ways that God had blessed them. If you remember from yesterday's lesson, we defined *blessing* as the happiness, joy, and sense of contentment that comes simply because God has touched one's life. Clearly, God touched the lives of the Israelites more than just once or twice. I wonder again if their story could have had a different outcome if they had just practiced remembering their blessings a little better? Here's the truth. Counting our blessings will help us navigate our present circumstances with grace and gratitude, even if we are faced with the most daunting crisis ever.

Some of you might be thinking, are we ever going to get back to Mary's story? The answer is yes. How does this all tie in? Mary experiences a few crises of her own. Let's read about one of them in Luke 2:1–7.

This passage may be familiar to you. If you have ever been to church on Christmas, you've certainly heard it before. It's easy to accept the story the text tells without giving a second thought to the characters' emotions and feelings, but let's really consider them now. Mary is *very* pregnant, has to travel three days (on foot and on a donkey) for a government-required census, and then, upon arrival, goes into labor with her firstborn, only to find out there is no room available. How would you have felt? Take a moment to reflect and write your thoughts below.

_____

_____

_____

Keep in mind, Mary does not have the perspective we do. We have the luxury of reading this text today with a clear picture of the full implications Jesus's life, death, and resurrection had for all of humanity. We understand that God intended His son to be born in a dingy barn, to be wrapped in burlap, to be surrounded by the unpleasant smell of animals, and to be virtually unnoticed by the general population. The poetic beauty of it suggests something profound and utterly spectacular about the character of our God. Mary, on the other hand, was faced with the messy and frightening task of giving birth in the most peculiar and outright unsanitary place. Do you think she ever wondered what God was up to? I certainly would have. Having my firstborn in the confines of a hospital with a nurse attending to my needs and an epidural for the pain was overwhelming enough for me.

Let's fast forward a bit to when Jesus is twelve. Read about what happened at the temple in Luke 2:41–49. Jesus is lost. For *three* days. Can you fathom the panic? Have your ever lost, or believed you lost, something or someone of high value? What were the circumstances and how did it make you feel?

_____

_____

_____

_____

I haven't lost a child, yet. I have four, so my day may come. There was a terrifying moment a few weeks ago, when I writing this very Bible study, that my computer froze mid-sentence. Computers do that from time to time, so I didn't melt down in a panicked puddle on the floor right away. I did, what we all do, when an electronic device acts strangely: I turned it off and then back on, hoping that would resolve the problem. It did restart, but soon after, the screen went black. There was nothing my extremely computer literate husband, nor I, could do to revive it. "It must be a battery issue," I thought. A day or so later, I sat at the Apple genius bar listening to my worst fears verbalized. "We'll send it away. I think I know what part shorted out, but there is a small chance you will lose your data," the technician told me. My heart beat out of my chest. I hadn't backed it up; I hadn't saved it to the cloud. The reality hit me like a ton of bricks. I had worked hundreds and hundreds of hours, and there was a distinct possibility it was all gone. It was horrifying.

I prayed a lot. I thought back and remembered the many times I had felt a pull in my spirit, a nagging at my heart, the words, "just write" on repeat bouncing around in my head. I recalled when one of my closest friends said, "Christy, you just need to write." There was no way to ignore the fact that this Bible study was a clear directive from God. I knew it, not just in my head, but in the depths of my spirit. So, I waited. I checked my phone constantly, hoping that if I stared at it for long enough the Apple technician would call and I would finally know my fate. The waiting was torturous, but all along I felt an overwhelming sense of peace. I knew that God would come through. He had been faithful to me many times before and I felt certain this would be no exception. If the file was gone, God would get me through rewriting the parts I had lost. I also felt sure that He was more than capable of preserving it. The lightning bolts have to report to Him (Job 38:35); surely, His jurisdiction extended to computers as well—that's what I told myself as least. A few days later, I sat at my desk, my computer returned to me. I nervously clicked on the file. To my delight, I found the entirety of the study unscathed and unharmed; every word was just as I had left it.

I know it wasn't *that* much of a crisis. It was certainly nothing like Mary had to endure. The truth is that whatever trials and tribulations we face and whatever catastrophes, big or small, we must go through, life always has a tendency to feel insurmountable. Let's reread the interaction Mary had with her son shortly after they found Him teaching in the temple (Luke 2:49–51). I think this will give us insight into how we, too, should respond in moments of crisis. Fill in the following blanks.

"But they did _____ what he was saying to them" (Luke 2:50 NIV).

"But his mother _____ all these things in her heart" (Luke 2:51b NIV).

Mary doesn't understand it, but she accepts it. She accepts it because, although she cannot see the full picture, she can be certain of one thing. God can be trusted. He has been faithful and He will be faithful again. Anything else would be a violation of His unwavering and steadfast character. "His mercy extends to those who fear him, from generation to generation" (Luke 1:50 NIV). Judging from Mary's reaction in these uncertain circumstances, she genuinely believed these words to be true. She was putting the trust she had in God into practice. We may never fully understand why tragedy befalls us, but we do have to resolve to accept it over time. We must learn to say, in the words of Jeremiah, as recorded in Lamentations 3:21–24:

> Yet this I call to mind
>   and therefore I have hope:
> Because of the Lord's great love we are not consumed,
>   for his compassions never fail.
> They are new every morning;
>   great is your faithfulness.
> I say to myself, "The Lord is my portion;
>   therefore I will wait for him" (NIV).

Let's all take a moment, as we close, to recall to mind some specific ways God's mercy has saved us from being consumed and how His compassions have never failed us. Let's allow our souls to be filled with hope once again. It's not easy to come to terms with the fact that we may never understand why certain things happen the way they do. Perhaps you are struggling or having trouble accepting something that has happened in your life or to someone you love. Perhaps you find it hard to trust God about it. Perhaps, right now, the only emotion you feel is anger. Perhaps your anger consumes you in a way that it is terrifying. You feel as though you are drowning in your own contempt and may never surface. Invite God into that anger. There is no safer space for you to unleash your emotions than with Him in prayer. He can handle everything you are going through and all that you feel. He cannot be offended. He can rescue you from whatever it is you feel you cannot escape from.

Day Four

AND A SWORD WILL
PIERCE YOUR OWN SOUL

For whoever wants to save his life will lose it, but whoever loses his life for me and for the gospel will save it. What good is it for man to gain the whole world, yet forfeit his very soul? Or what can a man give in exchange for his soul? (Mark 8:35–37 NIV).

Yesterday we spent some time in the text examining some of the predicaments in which Mary found herself. Despite what you might think, it wasn't always easy being the mother of God in the flesh. Having a Son who was carrying out the will of His divine Father had some major perks, but also posed some challenges. We know very little about Jesus's early life, but, I think it is safe to say, there were probably more than a few bumps in the road. I think Mary's habit of remembering what God had done for her in the past, as evidenced in the *Magnificat* we studied, gave her the hope and strength she needed to navigate the trials she encountered as the mother of Jesus. I also believe, that nothing, absolutely nothing, that she had ever experienced could have prepared her for the future, for the gut-wrenching and altogether devastating events that would unfold. Turn to Luke 2:22–35 and read what happens when Jesus is presented at the temple sometime in the first weeks of his life.

What is it that Simeon says to Mary about her son Jesus?

_____

_____

_____

These are not exactly words of comfort for a young mother already overwhelmed and exhausted by the demanding days and nights of taking care of a newborn baby, are they?

You never forget that first pregnancy. Every one is incredible and beautiful, but you never forget the joy of living every day with a miracle growing in your belly for the first time. Feeling the kicks and jabs of your little love is exhilarating, even though they can also be painful enough to take your breath away. And absolutely nothing compares to the joy you feel the second that sweet little life takes its first breath. I remember the moment as if it was yesterday. The nurses placed my firstborn on my chest, and I looked into his eyes. The first hours, and months, are somewhat of a blur, but I do remember the staring. Always staring. Always watching. Always awed. This tiny and perfect person belonged to me. I struggled to fathom the greatness of the gift. I watched him stretch, yawn, and strain to open his precious eyes, only to, ever so quickly, succumb back to sleep. I had been given a front row seat. In those early days it was to observe the peaceful slumber, but that would change. He would grow and I would be there for first laughs, first steps, first days of school, and for every other milestone in between. It is one of the finest gifts ever to be called a mother.

Have you had the joy of experiencing what I described above? Share some below. If you are not a mother, can you recall your own mother describing the joys of motherhood?

_____

_____

_____

That's the thing about motherhood. It's timeless and universal. Mary felt the same emotions that I did, the ones that bubbled to the surface and spilled over instantaneously at the sight of my firstborn. Mary may have experienced the same feelings, but we know she wasn't just any mother—she was the mother of God's Son. What a front row seat that would have been! Imagine that your son, the one you birthed and raised, whose tears you dried and whose boo boo's you kissed and made better, is now a grown man with thousands of followers. He's traveling from town to town, healing the leper, giving sight to the blind, making whole what's been broken. There would come a day when the sun would set on His days of ministry and rise on the moment that would change everything. Through all this, you've been His mother. Yes, I think "a sword piercing your heart" might be an accurate description, but it only scratches the surface of how you would truly feel. Read what happened John 19:16–27 and fill in the blank from verse 25: "Near the _____ stood his mother…" (NIV).

Jesus endured crucifixion, an unimaginably painful execution. His hands and feet were nailed to a cross; He was left to hang until void of any strength, crushed by the weight of own His body. As He took his final breath, she stood there. Mary watched it all. She must have had her heart ripped open and torn it into a million tiny pieces. My fellow mothers, can you even begin to fathom this?

For those who chose to follow Jesus, specifically for those closest to Him, there was a difficult and sobering reality to be faced. If you walked as He did and followed in His footsteps, the end of the road might just mean the end of your life. We are not immune to the same fate as the disciples attempting to live out His commandments in today's world. Many of us have the privilege of living in a country with rights such as freedom of speech and religion, but others are not quite so lucky. In John 15:18–16:4, Jesus warned His disciples of the risk involved in following Him. Read this passage and answer the following questions.

What reason did Jesus give for the world hating those who considered themselves His disciples?

_____

_____

_____

Why is it that we must face persecution, just as He did?

_____

_____

_____

Nearly all of Jesus's twelve disciples were killed because of their choice to follow Him. Some were beheaded, some crucified, some stoned to death, some banished, and some speared, but all were unable to escape the persecution Jesus promised would come.

There have been many more who have experienced the same fate. Dietrich Bonhoeffer, a writer and theologian, has inspired and challenged me with his teachings, not only because his words are filled with conviction, but because his actions are proof of his convictions. He was born in 1906 in Germany, and he received his theological degree from Tubingen University. He went on to travel, study, write, and preach all over the world. In the summer of 1933, a group called Deutsche Christian ("German Christian") began to echo the sentiments of Nazi ideology within the walls of the evangelical church. They advocated the removal of the Old Testament from the Holy Scriptures. Ultimately, they refused the right to any non-Aryan attempting to take on roles of leadership. As time went on, they banned them from attending church at all. Bonhoeffer wildly opposed these ideas and spent the remainder of his life fighting for the truth. He helped found an anti-Nazi church and established an underground seminary to further educate those who stood against Hitler. Eventually imprisoned and sent to Buchenwald, a concentration camp, he was ultimately hung when he was only thirty-nine years old. He and four members of his immediate family died at the hands of the Nazis.[1] In one of his most famous books, *The Cost of Discipleship*, Bonhoeffer says this, "When Christ calls a man, He bids him come and die."[2]

In Dietrich Bonhoeffer's struggle against the Nazis, persecution meant literal death. We may not face persecution exactly the same way living in North America. However,

---

1 Jewish Virtual Library: A Project of the American-Israeli Cooperative Enterprise, 2015, https://www.jewishvirtuallibrary.org/jsource/biography/Bonhoeffer.html.

2 Bonhoeffer, Dietrich, The Cost of Discipleship (New York, New York. Touchstone, 1959), 44.

persecution exists here, too. I have had the privilege of hanging out with and mentoring a young girl who is a part of our church's student ministry. She attends the public high school directly across the street from our church building, and recently, she and her twin sister have attempted to start a Christian club on campus. She explained to me, the other day as we met, just how shocked and surprised she was at the negativity, unkind words, and outright hatred that had been thrown their way by their fellow students. She was surprised by the responses they got because all they wanted to do was create a safe place on campus for their peers to come and explore faith. It happens, here and now. Jesus said, "If they persecuted me, they will persecute you also" (John 15:20 NIV). What is true then is also true now.

Have you ever experienced a time where you felt "persecuted" for what you believed? Keep in mind that this is just as much about emotional hurt as physical.

_____

_____

_____

There is pain involved in following Jesus. It is not only because of what others can do to us, but because of the battle that is being fought over our souls. Sometimes our greatest enemy is ourselves. Jesus said, "If anyone would come after me, let him deny himself and take up his cross and follow me" (Mark 8:34 ESV). Self-denial is never easy. Somewhere, buried in our core, is the belief that we should come first. We bow our knee to the god of self, and in the process, we sacrifice our souls. "For whoever wants to save their life will lose it, but whoever loses their life for me and for the gospel will save it. What good is it for someone to gain the whole world, yet forfeit their soul?" (Mark 8:35–36 NIV).

What does it mean to you to "lose your life"?

_____

_____

_____

Have you ever experienced true life as a result of dying for something or someone? Explain.

_____

_____

_____

Read Philippians 3:7–9. What things do you need to lose today? They might even be things that you considered profitable and good at one time or another.

_____

_____

_____

I want to close today with something else that Dietrich Bonhoeffer wrote. I hope it challenges you, as it did me.

> Costly grace is the gospel which must be sought again and again and again, the gift which must be asked for, the door at which a man must knock. Such grace is costly because it calls us to follow, and it is grace because it calls us to follow Jesus Christ. It is costly because it costs a man his life, and it is grace because it gives a man the only true life. It is costly because it condemns sin, and grace because it justifies the sinner. Above all, it is costly because it cost God the life of his Son: 'Ye were bought at a price', and what has cost God much cannot be cheap for us. Above all, it is grace because God did not reckon his Son too dear a price to pay for our life, but delivered him up for us. Costly grace is the Incarnation of God.[1]

1 Bonhoeffer, Dietrich, *The Cost of Discipleship* (Simon and Schuster, Aug 7, 2012 - Religion - page.45 –Kindle Edition)

Day Five

PONDER

But his mother treasured all these things in her heart (Luke 2:51 NIV).

We've made it. We've arrived. Today is the last and final day of our study together. I'm not sure that anyone is happier than I am. The words on these pages began years and years ago with a fascination I had with these five women whose names made it into Jesus's genealogy. These five blessed women don't just share a history with any ordinary man, they share one with God Himself. They were given key roles in the story that God was telling. They were a part of the revelation He is continuing to unfold through the lives of His people. He is relentless in His pursuit of redemption, buying back each life, and not giving up until we are all folded into His loving embrace. Each woman we have studied inhabited a different time. Each had their own challenges. Each of them was broken in some way, wrestling with their own set of demons, coming to terms with shortcomings, and learning to face their fears with courage and grace. Each of them, in spite of all their challenges was used uniquely by God to bring restoration to a broken world.

I wasn't sure how to close our journey, but I didn't have to look too far for inspiration. As always, the text gives us insight and becomes a light unto our paths. In this case, and quite appropriately, it is part of Mary's story that inspires our last day of study. If you would, turn to Luke 1:19, and then flip over to Luke 2:51. You will find a common phrase in both of these verses. Please write it below.

_____

As parents, we do this, don't we? We "ponder" and "treasure" the sweet, wonderful, hilarious, and even the aggravating things, that our children say and do. We watch them intently. We study their every move. We take great delight in considering the ways they learn. With each passing day, we note how they interact with the world around them. We observe how they are being shaped and formed into something special, beautiful, and unique. We take great pride in even the smallest accomplishments and gush over every triumph. It's what we do.

When Oliver was in his very first year of preschool, my husband and I attended back-to-school night. Our large bodies folded into pint-size chairs made for three- and four-year-olds. We stared up at his teacher, who seemed much larger and foreboding than she actually was with our newly realized and shrunken perspectives. She asked us to introduce ourselves and tell her which of the children were ours. "I'm Christy and this is Michael. We are Oliver's parents," I said.

"Oh," she responded, "Oliver! Yes, he's such a smart boy. He can already write his name so well. I'm not sure any of the others can do that quite yet." My heart felt like it was going to simply burst with pride.

Before I could contain myself, I blurted out with an obnoxious level of egotism over my firstborn, "Yes, he's *really* smart." There went my one chance at a good first impression with all the parents. I had now became *that* mother, the one that unabashedly gloats and boasts about their child. The kind that truly believes their offspring has superior genes to that of the rest of humanity. The one that doesn't know when to shut up. I was that person.

Later that night, as we lay in bed, I said to my husband, Michael, "I probably should have exerted a little more humility, perhaps reined in my excitement just a tad."

My husband responded, "Your enthusiasm was adorable, but, yes, you might have toned it down just a touch." He let me down easy, but the thought of that moment still makes me cringe with embarrassment.

I think Mary had it right. She pondered the accomplishments of her quite extraordinary son in her heart. I could have probably followed her example on back-to-school night. If anyone had an excuse to have a case of verbal diarrhea over their Son's abilities, it was Mary! Her offspring was literally supernatural, but she simply kept her thoughts about Him in her heart.

Our children do give us an especially great feeling of pride—one unsurpassed by any other thing in our lives. It's why we keep baby books and blogs. It's why we flood social media with pictures and lists of our child's most recent talents, adventures, and exploits. It might be why people "unfriend" or "unfollow" us from time to time just to hold onto their sanity. As a mother of four, I have to speak for all parents and tell you, we can't help it! We really can't. We love our children with a love so profound, it's shocking. As Anne Lamott wrote, "there really are places in your heart you don't even know exist until you love a child."[1] As parents, we simply did not know we had the capacity for this kind of love prior to our children's entrance into the world. To keep that love to ourselves, to water it down, as to not offend others, seems criminal—even impossible—at times.

It occurred to me, as I read these words repeatedly, "But Mary treasured up all these things and considered them in her heart" (Luke 2:19 NIV), that the pride we feel, the joy, the urge to remember and record ever detail, and the unimaginable love we feel for our children is what God feels for us. He studies us. We enrapture Him. We are the object of His affection. Paul put it this way in his letter to the Ephesians, "Long before he laid down earth's foundations, he had us in mind, had settled on us as the focus of his love" (Ephesians 1:3 MSG). We, as God's children, are the focus of His love.

We are lucky enough to have both sets of grandparents involved in our lives and the lives of our children. They volunteer to babysit. They help us with household projects, they buy diapers, wipes, and groceries. I haven't bought toilet paper for our house in years. My mother-in-law is my personal shopper, and whenever she comes over, she almost always has a new shirt, dress, or pair of jeans for one of the kids with her. Sometimes, if we are lucky, she shops for me and my husband, as well.

---

1 Lamott, Anne, Operating Instructions: A Journal of My Son's First Year (New York: Ballantine Books, 1993)

My mom and dad bought a cabin in the woods of Prescott just two hours from our homes in Scottsdale. They equipped it with an eight-person bunkhouse. "It will have enough room for each one of your kids to come up and bring a friend," my mom informed us with a sense of joy and excitement. In the last six months, they have built a treehouse, purchased a trampoline, installed all sorts of swinging and jungle gym apparatuses (for my American ninja warrior-obsessed boys), and connected a zip line from the top of the tree house to a landing platform (harness required, this thing isn't for the faint of heart). There's a basketball hoop, billions of toys, a hot tub on the exquisite wraparound deck. To say it's fantastic, is an understatement. They are top of the line grandparents. We are blessed beyond words.

We often ask both sets of grandparents why they are as good to us as they are. We often feel undeserving of the love and extravagant gifts they shower on us. We never really know how to appropriately thank them, or how to assure them of the deep level of gratitude we feel in our hearts for all the ways in which they love us. Frequently though, in response to our many thanks, I hear my father-in-law say, "The greatest gift you'll ever know is to have your children reach adulthood and have them ask you to be a part, an integral part, of their lives and the lives of their children. I've known no greater joy."

Isn't the only appropriate response to the extravagant love of God to invite Him in and to make Him an integral part of our lives? All He really wants is what any parent covets. He wants us—his children. He wants us to be as interested in Him as He is in us. As Mary intently watched her son, and as God studies and cares for us, may we watch. May we anticipate. May we search out. May we return His affection. May we pay attention to our God at work in our lives. As He breathes new life into the mundane of our daily dealings, He gives rest to our weary souls. He rejoices over us and our accomplishments–both large and small. May we treasure all those things, and the millions of other ways that God reveals His love to us, and makes Himself known. May we ponder them in our hearts.

Let's recall the ways in which God has moved in our lives over the weeks we have spent together. Let's ponder the ways in which God has been at work. Use the following questions to help you in this process.

What stands out to you the most from the last six weeks?

_____

_____

Is there one woman and her story that spoke into your life more than any of the others?

_____

_____

_____

Was there a specific Scripture or phrase from His Word that has drawn you in? What is it and what has it stirred up inside of you?

_____

_____

_____

Is God currently leading you to make any specific changes in your life? Perhaps it is a specific habit or patterns that He desires to curtail or cultivate.

_____

_____

_____

Do you have any other thoughts, ideas, notes, or scribbles?

_____

_____

_____

A long time ago, when I was quite young, someone told me of the importance of keeping journals. "When you sense God doing something in your life—whatever it is—write it down," they said. Digging through some books the other day, I stumbled across some of my old journals from junior high and high school. I had verses written out, names of people God was leading me to invest in, prayers filled with praises, and many pages permeated with requests for forgiveness. The inmost desires of my heart are all bared on those pages. It's all there—a record of the relationship my God and I have shared together. I've come a long way since then, in some ways, but in other ways, I am the same. Once a child, now an adult, but, still and forevermore, His child.

If there is one final thought I want to leave you with and one truth I pray you cling to, it is that I hope you know, in the depth of your soul, He is pursuing you. He has been pursuing you. His mind has settled on you as the focus of His love, long before the foundations of the earth were laid. And He is everywhere. In the cool breeze brushing across your cheek, in the warmth of the sun, in the laughter of a friend, in the eyes of your child, in the dirty dishes in the sink, in the line at the grocery store, in the heartache of loss, and in the disappointment of missed expectations. He is everywhere. His eyes are on us. Let us turn our eyes towards Him. Let us give Him the only thing He truly desires. Let us make Him the focus of our love. Blessings to you. I am grateful to you for allowing me to be a part of your journey.

Video Session Seven
DEVOUT

SALVATION (LUKE 2:31-32)

Salvation comes in two distinct ways:

1) The _____ of your people _____.

2) The _____ for the revelation of the _____.

LESSONS FROM SIMEON (LUKE 2:25-32)

In the King James Version, that word for *righteous* is "devout." *Strong's Bible Concordance* defines the word devout as "to hold well, _____; and signifies care as to the realization of the presence and claims of God, reverencing God, pious, devout which manifests itself in caution and carefulness in human relationship. This one is an anxious and scrupulous worshipper who never changes or omits anything because he is afraid of _____."[1]

Luke 2:25–27 says, "Now there was a man in Jerusalem called Simeon, who was righteous and devout. He was waiting for the consolation of Israel, and the Holy Spirit was on him. It had been _____ to him by the _____ _____ that he would not die before he had seen the Lord's Messiah. _____ by the Spirit he went into the temple courts…" (NIV).

---

1 Strong, James, LL.D., S.T.D., "The New Strong's Expanded Exhaustive Bible Concordance of the Bible.' Thomas Nelson Publishers. 2010. 2126.

SIMEON'S PROPHETIC WORDS (LUKE 2:33-35)

"This child is destined to cause the _____ and _____ of many in Israel, and to be a sign spoken against, so that the thoughts of many hearts will be _____. And a sword will pierce your own soul too" (Luke 2:34–35 NIV).

SMALL GROUP
DISCUSSION GUIDE

On the following pages you will find questions from each
week of homework to guide your discussions.

Week One
SUBTEXT: FIVE WOMEN IN THE LINEAGE OF JESUS

REVIEW QUESTIONS

Day 1: What two men are described as major players in Jesus's genealogy?

Day 2: What nationality were each of the five women found in Matthew 1?

Day 3: According to Ephesians 1:3–10, what is the "mystery of His will" that is made known to us?

Day 4: Who was it that handed down to us the "empty ways of life" according to 1 Peter 1:18–19?

Day 5: Read Ephesians 2:19–22 as a group. Who is the chief cornerstone?

PERSONAL REFLECTION QUESTIONS

Day 1: Is there someone in your family tree that you, or your family, take a special interest in? If so, why might that be?

Day 2: Have you ever received news that shocked you or surprised you—something extremely unexpected, positive or negative, that ultimately altered your future?

Day 3: Is there any one person (this might be a family member, someone from work, a neighbor) that drives you crazy? How would your interactions with this person change if you began to see them as God does?

Day 4: Can you identify with the gerbil we discussed—feeling as though you are running and working very hard, but not actually getting anywhere?

Day 5: Can you draw any connections between the lives of the family that preceded you and your life today? Have those connections brought good or bad fruit to your life?

Week Two
PERIPETEIA: TAMAR

REVIEW QUESTIONS

Day 1:   Read Leviticus 20:7. What does the beginning of the verse tell the Israelites to do?

Day 2:   Review the list of rules you created from Exodus 20:1–17. Be sure to share with one another why you felt God might have established each of the rules listed.

Day 3:   What does it say that Tamar does in verses 13–14?

Day 4:   When Judah learns that Tamar is pregnant, what is his response?

Day 5:   See Genesis 3:7–13. What do both Adam and Eve do when confronted by God to give an account for their actions?

PERSONAL REFLECTION QUESTIONS

Day 1:   Are there any obstacles that stand in the way of you and your fellow believers being "one"? If so, what kind of steps do you need to take today to work towards reconciliation?

Day 2:   Have you ever felt burdened by a set of rules imposed on you either in the church or in some other context?

Day 3:   In what areas of your life are you most likely to try to take matters into your own hands?

Day 4:   Has your guilt and pride ever led you to shift unnecessary blame on others?

Day 5:   Do you see yourself in Eve and Tamar? What kinds of things do you put your hope in, believing they will bring you what you desire, only to be disappointed?

Week Three
OXYMORON: RAHAB

REVIEW QUESTIONS

Day 1:   What details outlined in the story of Rahab hint that God was behind the scenes orchestrating the partnership between our heroine and the spies?

Day 2:   What did Rahab use to hide the spies?

Day 3:   If you feel comfortable, share what you believe Rahab's inner monologue may have been.

Day 4:   What declarative statement does Rahab make in Joshua 2:11?

Day 5:   According to Joshua 2:18, what color cord was it that the spies requested Rahab to tie in the window of her home?

PERSONAL REFLECTION QUESTIONS

Day 1:   Have you ever had a situation where the events seemed like happenstance, but in hindsight, you clearly saw that God was at work?

Day 2:   Do you believe that God can use small and menial tasks for His purposes?

Day 3:   Can you identify ways in which you might be so well adjusted to your culture that you fit into it without even thinking?

Day 4:   Have you ever come to a place where you knew you just didn't have it in you to carry on without crying out for help?

Day 5:   How can you run into the Light while facing the particular circumstances surrounding you today?

Week Four
FORESHADOWING: RUTH

REVIEW QUESTIONS

Day 1:   What do the words, daughters and wept, tell us about the relationship between Naomi and her two daughters-in-law?

Day 2:   What specific adjective is used to describe Boaz?

Day 3:   What does Naomi hope her daughters-in-law will find?

Day 4:   Reading 2 Corinthians 5:17–21, consider how God provided our ultimate protection and shelter through Jesus, the culmination of all His promises.

Day 5:   How does life come full circle for Naomi?

PERSONAL REFLECTION QUESTIONS

Day 1:   Psalm 34:18 says, "If your heart is broken, you'll find God right there. If you're kicked in the gut, he'll help you catch your breath" (MSG). Have you ever experienced this to be true or witnessed its truth in the life of someone you know?

Day 2:   What words or phrase stands out to you from Romans 3:6–8?

Day 3:   Do you now have, or have you ever had, a person in your life you felt you could trust and were comfortable revealing even your most intimate vulnerabilities with?

Day 4:   How can you be "Christ's ambassador" living out the message of reconciliation today?

Day 5:   What were some of the blessings you recorded in the final activity of this week's homework?

Week Five
EPITHET: URIAH'S WIFE

REVIEW QUESTIONS

Day 1: In light of what we studies this week, what does Galatians 5:25 encourage us to do?

Day 2: Review the list you created of all the ways David schemes and carefully plots his cover-up.

Day 3: What does God's discipline produce in us?

Day 4: How does David reply when asked by his advisors why he has stopped his mourning?

Day 5: Read 1 Kings 1:11. When Nathan goes to Bathsheba, what does he ask her to do?

PERSONAL REFLECTION QUESTIONS

Day 1: Can you recall a time in your life when you fell out of step? Perhaps, in hindsight, you see clearly how that one misstep was the catalyst for the events that followed.

Day 2: Turn to Psalm 32:3–4. How does David describe his emotional state in these verses? Have you ever felt this way? If so, describe your feelings.

Day 3: Is your life characterized by ingratitude or gratitude?

Day 4: Do you ever find it hard to say "I'm sorry"? Is there a specific instance that comes to mind?

Day 5: How is God calling you to intercede and be an advocate for your loved ones or even for those you do not know?

Week Six
RISING ACTION: MARY

REVIEW QUESTIONS

Day 1:   Review the blanks you filled in from Luke 1:38.

Day 2:   What word does Elizabeth use to describe Mary on three separate occasions?

Day 3:   Review the two challenging circumstances that Mary endured, which were highlighted in today's lesson. Reference Luke 2:1–7 and Luke 2:41–49.

Day 4:   What is it that Simeon says to Mary about her son, Jesus?

Day 5:   What common phrase do you find in Luke 1:19 and Luke 2:51?

PERSONAL REFLECTION QUESTIONS

Day 1:   Can you recall a time in your life when you said yes in spite of your fears? Is there something you feel God is calling to say yes to—even though the thought it is making your palms clammy and your armpits sweat?

Day 2:   Share the list of blessings that you created at the end of today's lesson.

Day 3:   Have you ever lost, or believed you lost, something or someone of extremely high value? What were the circumstances and how did it make you feel?

Day 4:   Have you ever experienced a time where you felt persecuted for what you believed? Keep in mind that this is just as much about emotional pain as it is physical.

Day 5:   What stands out to you most from the last six weeks?

Scripture Memorization

EPHESIANS 1:1–12

I must confess that I am not always the best at the discipline of memorizing Scripture. It's not that I don't want to or can't. I'm just not always intentional about it. One of my favorite things about being in a Bible study with a small group of women is the accountability it provides. Knowing that I will be sitting around the table and looking into the eyes of my peers at the end of each week of study, makes me more committed to my homework. And knowing that I will actually have to say aloud what I have memorized to at least one person, forces me to stop making excuses and just do it. I have included this Scripture memorization guide for those who *want* to follow along with it week to week. The key being *want to*, or even better, feel led to by the Lord. If you do feel led to memorize the verses from Ephesians below, I encourage you to find one person in your small group that will hold you accountable. Perhaps you want to check in with one another on a weekly basis, or maybe you just want to say the verses aloud on the concluding day of the study. I'll let you decide.

I've chosen this particular passage of Scripture out of Ephesians because it speaks specifically about God's blessings. Sometimes we allow our brokenness to define who we are as opposed to letting God's truth take the dominant role in shaping us. As we study together, let's swap brokenness for blessings. Let's hide His words in our hearts, so no matter how loud the lies are that echo around us, His voice will be louder.

Week One

How blessed is God! And what a blessing he is! He's the Father of our Master, Jesus Christ, and takes us to the high places of blessing in him. Long before he laid down earth's foundations, he had us in mind, had settled on us as the focus of his love, to be made whole and holy by his love (Ephesians 1:3–4 MSG).

Week Two

Long, long ago he decided to adopt us into his family through Jesus Christ. (What pleasure he took in planning this!) He wanted us to enter into the celebration of his lavish gift-giving by the hand of his beloved Son (Ephesians 1:5–6 MSG).

Week Three

Because of the sacrifice of the Messiah, his blood poured out on the altar of the Cross, we're a free people—free of penalties and punishments chalked up by all our misdeeds. And not just barely free, either. Abundantly free! (Ephesians 1:7–8 MSG).

Week Four

He thought of everything, provided for everything we could possibly need, letting us in on the plans he took such delight in making (Ephesians 1:8–9a MSG).

Week Five

He set it all out before us in Christ, a long-range plan in which everything would be brought together and summed up in him, everything in deepest heaven, everything on planet earth (Ephesians 1:9b–10 MSG).

Week Six

It's in Christ that we find out who we are and what we are living for. Long before we first heard of Christ and got our hopes up, he had his eye on us, had designs on us for glorious living, part of the overall purpose he is working out in everything and everyone (Ephesians 1:11–12 MSG).

Week Seven

It's in Christ that you, once you heard the truth and believed it (this Message of your salvation), found yourselves home free—signed, sealed, and delivered by the Holy Spirit. This signet from God is the first installment on what's coming, a reminder that we'll get everything God has planned for us, a praising and glorious life (Ephesians 1:13–14 MSG).

ABOUT THE AUTHOR

Christy Fay lives in Scottsdale, Arizona where she and her husband pastor together. She married Michael, her high school sweetheart, and together they have four children: Oliver, Wesley, Crosby and Abby. Christy graduated from the University of San Diego with a degree in Education, minoring in Theology. She is passionate about the study and teaching of the Word of God and wants all women to uncover their true worth as daughters of the King.

Ever felt tossed aside or written off as useless or worthless?
Ever felt like you didn't quite belong?
Ever wondered if your life mattered?

The unlikely and surprising presence of five women in the genealogy of Jesus teach us an important and life-changing lesson. They are proof that there is nothing we have done that can ever disqualify us from a life chosen and used by God, a life that is reclaimed. We are all women of worth. We are all daughters of the King.

If you're a fan of this book, please tell others...

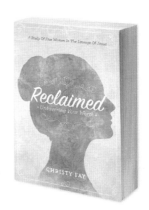

- Write about *Reclaimed—Uncovering Your Worth* on your blog, Facebook and Twitter.

- Suggest the book to your friends, neighbors and family.

- When you're in a bookstore, ask them if they carry the *Reclaimed—Uncovering Your Worth* study. This book is available through all major distributors, so any bookstore that does not have this book can easily stock it !

- Write a positive review of *Reclaimed—Uncovering Your Worth* on www.amazon.com

Connect With Us...

- To order more copies and or learn more about Christy Fay and *Reclaimed—Uncovering Your Worth* , go to **christyfay.com**.

STARFISH MENTORSHIP PROGRAM

Starfish Partnerships launched in January of 2014 with the goal of creating positive relationships for individuals who are exiting prostitution by creating a supportive relationship to help individuals achieve their own goals. The program includes one-on-one mentorship, monthly group meetings, and quarterly family events. Monthly meetings include a shared a meal and discuss relevant topics to support healthy lives, personal success, and ways to connect with your community.

There are between 14,500 and 17,500 people that are trafficked in the U.S. alone each year. Slavery is alive and well in our modern day and as followers of Jesus we are called to care for the victims and fight this injustice.

Find out more about Starfish Mentorship Program and how your donation can help.

Starfish Mentor Program
602-258-2785
starfishpartnerships@gmail.com

MY PRAYER PACKAGES

Reclaiming God's Love Through Gifts

Prayer Packages
Bundled Christian Gifts. Delivered

Shop Online:
myprayerpackages.com